STANDARD GRADE & INTERMEDIATE I
Physical Education
course notes

✕ Malcolm Thorburn ✕

Text © 2005 Malcolm Thorburn
Design & layout © 2005 Leckie & Leckie Ltd.
Cover image © Joe Polillio/Getty-Stone

04/150508

ISBN 978-1-84372-357-8

Published by:
Leckie & Leckie
3rd Floor
4 Queen Street
Edinburgh
EH2 1JE

Tel: 0131 220 6831
Fax: 0131 225 9987

enquiries@leckieandleckie.co.uk
www.leckieandleckie.co.uk

Special thanks to:
BRW (creative packaging), Caleb Rutherford (cover design), Pumpkin House
(concept design and illustration), Jim Ferguson (content review), Roda
Morrison (copy-editing), Scottish Rugby (foreword) and Tara Watson
(proofreading).

We would like to thank Getty images for permission to reproduce the
following photographs:
© Getty/Timothy A. Clary-Stringer (p. 19)
© Getty/Michael Steele-Staff (p. 19)
© Getty/David Rogers-Staff (p.31 & p62)
© Getty/Kim Jae-Hwan-Staff (p. 47)
© Getty/Carl De Souza-Stringer (p. 47)
© Getty/Warren Little-Staff (p. 49)
© Getty/Mark Dadswell-Staff (p. 49)
© Getty/Alexander Hassenstein-Staff (p. 49)
© Getty/Javier Soriano-Staff (p. 50)
© Getty/Nadine Rupp-Stringer (p. 51)
© Getty/Brian Bahr-Staff (p. 62)
© Getty/China Photos-Stringer (p. 63)
© Getty/Ramzi Haidar-Staff (p. 75)
© Getty/Clive Brunskill-Staff (p. 87)
© Getty/Clive Brunskill-Staff (p. 87)
© Getty/Jonathan Ferrey-Staff (p. 96)
© Getty/Robert Laberge-Staff (p. 98)

A CIP Catalogue record for this book is available from the British Library.

® Leckie & Leckie is a registered trademark

Leckie & Leckie Ltd is a division of Huveaux plc.

CONTENTS

FOREWORD

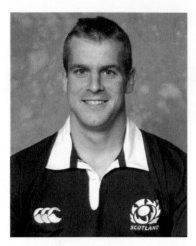

For me, physical education was the most complete subject in school. It offered strong core values in a fun way that, in my opinion, no other class could. PE inspired discipline through respect for officials and referees, for rules and laws and for fellow teammates and competitors. Teamwork and cooperation were hugely important values; again represented in sport and physical education.

Winning and losing games and competitions teach us which values we hold as individuals. A competitive spirit in life is invaluable, and PE offers exposure to the joy of winning and, more importantly, how to react to the pain of losing. These values have certainly helped me in my career - although the losing part never gets any easier than it did at school!

As well as all those practical issues, PE offers great depth in knowledge and understanding. This knowledge provides an enjoyment of watching and participating in sport at all levels which is vital if any of you want to pursue a career in sport.

With the help of this new book, I hope you will take the opportunity to relate your practical experiences to areas of knowledge and understanding and evaluation. A grasp of these areas will help you improve your performance. Take time to read and review your progress and check your understanding. This will help you develop your potential and set new targets for you to work towards.

Selecting Standard Grade Physical Education as a course option can help you in many ways. It shows that you are interested in your fitness and well-being; it shows that you enjoy working with others, giving feedback, offering encouragement and so on. It shows that you can play fair. These are great personal qualities to have as a student growing up, and they will serve you well in life and in sport if you wish to perform at a higher level.

Above all though, all of these standards and values are provided to us through PE in the best way possible – having fun.

Chris Paterson

Edinburgh Rugby

INTRODUCTION

INTRODUCTION

Welcome

Standard Grade Physical Education is about **your** active participation in a broad range of physical activities. Through active participation you work and learn with your class in a range of different roles: performer, observer, and through working co-operatively and in competition with other pupils.

These *Course Notes* are designed to help you understand Standard Grade Physical Education.

Standard Grade Physical Education is useful:

- ▸ for your own interest and self-development
- ▸ as a subject to add breadth and balance to your other subjects
- ▸ as part of your progression towards studying Physical Education as part of Higher Still Physical Education

Standard Grade Physical Education is made up of three assessable areas. These are:

Practical Performance   Knowledge and Understanding   Evaluating

Course outline

Practical Performance

Your course will involve you participating in a range of different types (categories) of activities. Some of these activities may be new to you and others will be familiar to you. The different activities chosen will reflect the facilities and options possible for your school. Your course will involve activities from a minimum of five categories of activities. Examples of some of the specific activities which might be offered are set out below.

CATEGORIES								
i	ii	iii	iv	v	vi	vii	viii	ix
Gymnastics	Dance	Water-based activities	Outdoor pursuits	Individual activities Directly competitive	Individual activities Indirectly competitive	Team games: Indoor	Team games: Outdoor	Thematic study
Modern	Ethnic	**Swimming**	Orienteering	**Badminton**	Archery	Basketball	**Hockey**	Fitness
Olympic	**Modern**	Life-saving	Hillwalking	Tabletennis	Trampoline	**Volleyball**	Football	Performance
Rhythmic	Contemporary	Canoeing	Skiing	Tennis	Athletics	Netball	Rugby	Movement

The activities in bold in the diagram above provide an example Standard Grade course (as shown opposite).

Olympic Gymnastics	Modern Dance	Swimming	Badminton	Volleyball	Hockey

Make a note of the different activities in your Standard Grade course.

Improving your performance

To improve your performance you work on basic movement patterns, specific skills, and applying skills when taking part in full performance - for example, when completing gymnastics floor sequences and taking part in competitive team games.

You can help yourself to improve performance both during your course and outside school. In school you can:

▸ Work out your strengths and weaknesses in each of the activities in your course

▸ Compare your performance against pupils in your class

▸ Be receptive to feedback from your teacher

▸ Try to set realistic improvement targets

▸ Try to make performance improvements in all activities in your course (not just in your favourite activities)

Outside school you can:

▸ Continue to practise your skills

▸ Ensure your fitness level is good

▸ Take part in different sports, as part of the extended school day and in your local community

Knowledge and Understanding

Your course will involve you studying three areas within Knowledge and Understanding. These are: Activities; the Body; and Skills and Techniques.

Activities: involves you studying the nature and purpose of different categories of activities, the official / formal and unwritten rules which define activities, and various roles and functions within activities.

The Body: involves you studying the structure and function of the human body, different aspects of fitness and training, and their effects.

Skills and Techniques: involves you studying concepts of skills and techniques, ways of developing a skill, and mechanical principles which underpin effective performance.

These three areas are covered in detail from pages 17 to 98.

INTRODUCTION

Improving your knowledge and understanding

To improve knowledge and understanding you will adopt different roles during your course. For example, when you are working on your performance you need to select and apply different skills and techniques at certain times: you need to put into practice what you are working on during lessons. You will also be involved in giving feedback; for example, to a partner after you have been working in pairs on performance related tasks.

You can help yourself to improve knowledge and understanding both during your course and outside school. In school you can:

> ▸ Link information about areas of knowledge and understanding ('Activities', 'the Body', and 'Skills and Techniques') with improving practical performance in the activities in your course
>
> ▸ Link new information to different categories of activities to broaden your understanding
>
> ▸ Deepen your understanding by completing all roles in your course – performing, acting as official, analysing your partner practising a skill, recording - to the best of your ability

Outside school you can:

> ▸ Observe and analyse different sports and different areas of knowledge and understanding in your local community and on television

Evaluating

Your course will involve you evaluating performance by observing and describing sporting actions in different activities and suggesting improvements. This will involve you recognising basic actions, observing fitness levels and studying in detail different techniques and how they affect the development of quality performance. This area is covered in greater detail on pages 100 to 101.

Improving your evaluating

Improving your evaluating abilities will help you compare performances against specific criteria, as well as define criteria for effective evaluation. Different methods of analysis are possible: occasionally you will observe and describe the efficiency of movement; at other times you might study body shape and the use of space; and at other times the preparation, action and recovery involved in different techniques. For effective evaluating try to make sure your comments are relevant, accurate, as detailed as possible and positive.

You can help yourself to improve your evaluating abilities both during your course and outside school. In school you can:

> ▸ Observe in detail, train your eyes to take in information and make considered suggestions for improvement
>
> ▸ Observe, describe and suggest improvement in different categories of activities to broaden your analytical abilities
>
> ▸ Deepen your understanding by regularly reviewing performance against different criteria, for example, fitness qualities as well as technique

Outside school you can:

> ▸ Observe and analyse different sports in your local community and on television

Integrated Performance, Knowledge and Understanding and Evaluation

The intention in Standard Grade is that different course areas are integrated. For example, as well as trying to improve performance you might also be trying to improve 'Skills and Techniques' as part of your knowledge and understanding study. Similar links will exist between performance and evaluation. An integrated course example is shown below.

Activities	Assessment Outcomes			Year
	PP	KU	EV	
Olympic Gymnastics	✓		✓	S3 & S4
Modern Dance	✓	✓		S3
Swimming	✓	✓		S3 & S4
Badminton	✓	✓	✓	S3 & S4
Volleyball		✓	✓	S3 & S4
Hockey	✓		✓	S4

In these *Course Notes* different pictures are used to highlight performance in activities. The purpose of these pictures is to illustrate information in the text and prompt you to ask questions which will help deepen your understanding of why knowledge can play a part in improving your performance.

For example: Which physical aspect of fitness do you most need to be a midfielder in football?

Answer: Cardiorespiratory endurance

What is cardiorespiratory endurance? It is whole body endurance, where the heart and lungs are required to help the body work aerobically with oxygen for long periods of time.

Why is cardiorespiratory endurance necessary for midfield players in football? It is necessary because midfield players need to keep running for the whole game.

Make a note of the different activities and assessment outcomes for your course.

Course Assessment

The three course areas (Performance, Knowledge and Understanding and Evaluating) are assessed in different ways.

Practical Performance

Your performance abilities will be assessed in a minimum of four different activities from your course. You will be assessed continuously as your course progresses. Your teacher(s) will give you feedback about your performance in different activities throughout your course.

To pass at **foundation level** you need to perform **basic skills** and link these together in a mostly effective way.

To pass at **general level** you need to perform **basic skills** and **make related judgements**

To pass at **credit level** you need to perform **complex skills** and adapt and combine skills in contexts involving a **wide variety of options**.

INTRODUCTION

Badminton example

Consider the following badminton shots. Some are basic skills and others are complex skills. To gain a foundation performance mark you need to carry out many of the basic skill shots. To gain a general performance mark you need to carry out the basic skill shots as well as some of the complex skill shots. To gain a credit mark you need to perform many of the complex skills with control and fluency plus all the basic skill shots consistently well.

Basic skill shots	Complex skill shots
High serve	Low and flick serves
Overhead clear	Overhead drop shot
Underarm clear	Net shot
	Backhand clear
	Overhead smash

Knowledge and understanding

Your knowledge and understanding is assessed as part of an examination at the end of your course. The content which forms pages 17 to 98 in the *Course Notes* forms the basis of the questions asked in the examination.

To pass at **foundation level** you need to show limited relevant knowledge and understanding of facts and principles.

To pass at **general level** you need to show a **greater range** of relevant knowledge and understanding of facts and principles.

To pass at **credit level** you need to show **detailed** knowledge and understanding and the ability to **interpret** facts and principles.

Consider the following examples of questions on 'Tactics and Strategies'.

A

Name one benefit of using a tactic in a game.

B

Choose one team activity. Name one role you had in that activity. Describe a defensive responsibility and an attacking responsibility that went with this role. An example answer is provided.

Activity: **Basketball**   *Role:* **Guard**

Defensive responsibility: I had to make sure I kept my 'opposite number' away from our basket. The closer she came, the more pressure I put her under.

Attacking responsibility: I had to help set up our attacking plays by passing to different players. I also took some 'outside' shots if I wasn't being marked and other options were not available.

Defensive responsibility:

Attacking responsibility:

C

Choose a tactic from a team activity. Explain, in detail, how the tactic chosen was well suited for both your individual and team strengths. An example answer is provided.

Activity: **Badminton (doubles)**

Tactic: **Playing 'sides' when defending**

Description: **When defending, I have good court movement. This helps me move forward and back to play different shots. In addition, my partner is of similar ability to me. As a result, we do not have a weak side which our opponents can exploit by hitting to it when the chance arises.**

Description:

Question A is a foundation level question, as you need to outline one benefit of using a tactic in a game. Question B is a general level question, as you need to show a greater range of knowledge and understanding by linking and describing attacking and defensive responsibilities in a chosen activity. Question C is a credit level question as you need interpret how the tactic chosen links to your own individual and team strengths.

Evaluating

Your evaluating ability is assessed as part of an examination at the end of your course.

To pass at **foundation level** you need to identify and describe in **basic** terms different actions and make **some** suggestions to improve performance.

To pass at **general level** you need to **identify and describe** different actions and make some suggestions to improve performance.

To pass at **credit level** you need to identify and describe **in detail** different actions and make some **detailed** suggestions to improve performance.

Here is an example of an evaluating question (parts a and b).

(a) Describe, in the correct order, four movements of the attacking player.

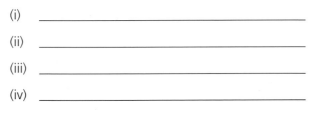

    (i)   _____

    (ii)   _____

    (iii) _____

    (iv) _____

(b) Suggest two improvements the attacker could make to improve her chance of scoring.

    (i)   _____

    (ii)   _____

In your evaluating examination you will gain marks at **foundation level** if you can identify skills such as **'passing'** and **'catching'**. To gain further marks at **general level** it is useful if you can add further details such as the type of pass and the direction of the pass; for example, in basketball **'chest pass forward** to team mate'. To gain further marks at **credit level** you need to add further detail to your descriptions such as '**fast** chest pass forward to team mate'.

Evaluating and knowledge and understanding examination

Based on your progress during your course and after discussions with your teacher(s) you will either complete the evaluating and knowledge and understanding examination at foundation and general level **or** general and credit level. The examination lasts approximately 55 minutes at all levels.

The examination question paper is in two parts: Section 1 is on evaluating and Section 2 is on knowledge and understanding. All questions are in two parts and you answer both parts of each question. For the video based evaluating questions you will hear a commentary throughout the video which provides instructions about how and when to answer questions. You will have time to practise answering these types of questions during your course.

Course weighting

Performance counts for 50% of your final mark, with knowledge and understanding (25%) and evaluating (25%) making up the other 50% of your final mark. When you have completed all parts of your assessment successfully you will be awarded either an overall foundation, general or credit level award.

What these Course Notes cover

These *Course Notes* are divided into five sections. The first three sections provide you with valuable information about the three main areas of knowledge and understanding in Standard Grade: Activities, the Body, and Skills and Techniques. Some notes cover credit level Standard Grade in particular and these are labelled clearly. The sections also contain revision 'Quicksmart' questions and 'Put into Practice' suggestions. Section 4 contains further information about evaluating in Standard Grade and Section 5 provides further details about Intermediate 1 Level Physical Education.

Intermediate 1 Physical Education

These *Course Notes* are also designed to help you understand Intermediate 1 Level Physical Education, an award which has similar aims to Standard Grade Physical Education.

Unit / Course Outline and Assessment

Higher Still qualifications are made up of **Units** and **Course awards**.

Two Units make up a Course award at Intermediate 1 Level. These are:

    Performance Unit

    Analysis and Development of Performance Unit

Performance Unit

You agree the activities for your Unit and Course with your teacher and class colleagues. As you develop your skills as a performer your teacher will give you feedback on how well you are improving. You can also use your free time to develop your ability. Try to set realistic improvement targets.

Your teacher assesses you in the different activities. He or she will give you details about your level of performance and tell you when it is at the required level to achieve the Unit. If you achieve the Performance Unit, you can use it as part of your Course award in Physical Education. You will take part in a minimum of four activities in a Course, but only two activities are required for the assessment of your Performance.

You can achieve a Unit at a level above that in which you are completing a Course award. This allows you to gain credit for your achievement. It may be, for example, that you could get credit for having achieved a Course award overall at Intermediate 1, while gaining extra Unit credit for having achieved the Unit in Performance at Intermediate 2 Level.

Analysis And Development Of Performance Unit

The four areas of **Analysis and Development of Performance** are:

▶ Area 1   Performance Appreciation
▶ Area 2   Preparation of the Body
▶ Area 3   Skills and Techniques
▶ Area 4   Structures, Strategies and Composition

Your Analysis and Development of Performance will include the study of at least three of these areas. Each of these areas of Analysis and Development of Performance is made up of a number of **Key Concepts**. These are briefly outlined below. On page 103 you can see where these *Course Notes* make specific links between the different areas of knowledge and understanding in Standard Grade and the Key Concepts at Intermediate 1 level.

Performance Appreciation (Area 1)

is a **general** broad view of performance which relates to the three other specific areas of analysis of performance areas. The Key Concepts in this area are:

- Overall nature and demands of quality performance
- Technical, physical, personal and special qualities of performance
- Mental factors influencing performance
- Use of appropriate models of performance
- Planning and managing personal performance improvement

Preparation of the Body (Area 2)

is a **specific** analysis of the fitness and training requirements necessary for your performance. The Key Concepts in this area are:

- Fitness assessment in relation to personal performance and the demands of activities
- Application of different types of fitness in the development of activity specific performance
- Physical, skill-related and mental types of fitness
- Principles and methods of training
- Planning, implementing and monitoring training

Skills and Techniques (Area 3)

is a **specific** analysis of your skills and techniques needs in performance. The Key Concepts in this area are:

- The concept of skill and skilled performance
- Skill / technique improvement through mechanical analysis or movement analysis or consideration of quality
- The development of skill and the refinement of technique

INTRODUCTION

Structures, Strategies and Composition (Area 4)

is a **specific** analysis of the influence of shape, form and design on your performance. The Key Concepts in this area are:

- The structures, strategies and / or compositional elements that are fundamental to activities

- Identification of strengths and weaknesses in performance in terms of:
  – roles and relationships, formations, tactical or design elements, choreography and composition

- Information processing, problem-solving and decision-making when working to develop and improve performance

---

Integrated teaching and learning

In Intermediate 1 Level Physical Education performance in different activities is integrated with different areas of Analysis and Development of Performance. The example below shows the links between Performance in basketball and Analysis and Development of Performance in Preparation of the Body: it shows how performing in basketball links with studying the different Key Concepts in Preparation of the Body.

Aims: to improve basketball performance

to improve my understanding of Preparation of the Body

'We played small-sided basketball game to establish level of general fitness for basketball'	The accurate recording of data in standard tests or full performance contexts
'We adopted different roles in small-sided games and studied the different specific fitness needs for each type of role – guard, forward and centre'	The differences between general and specific fitness in basketball
'The centres needed strength and speed when rebounding'	The need for strength and speed (physical fitness)
'The forwards needed agility and co-ordination when driving to the basket to complete lay up shot'	The need for agility and co-ordination (skill-related fitness)
'The guards needed to manage emotion and rehearse attacking plays when bringing the ball out of defense'	The need for managing emotion and rehearsal (mental fitness)
'We set up a circuit with different exercises in it to improve strength and speed'	Set up an interval training programme to develop strength and speed
'We completed game analysis sheets which help show whether we were getting fitter and whether our interval training had been effective'	Monitor progress as training progresses

Outcomes: improved basketball performance

improved understanding of Preparation of the Body

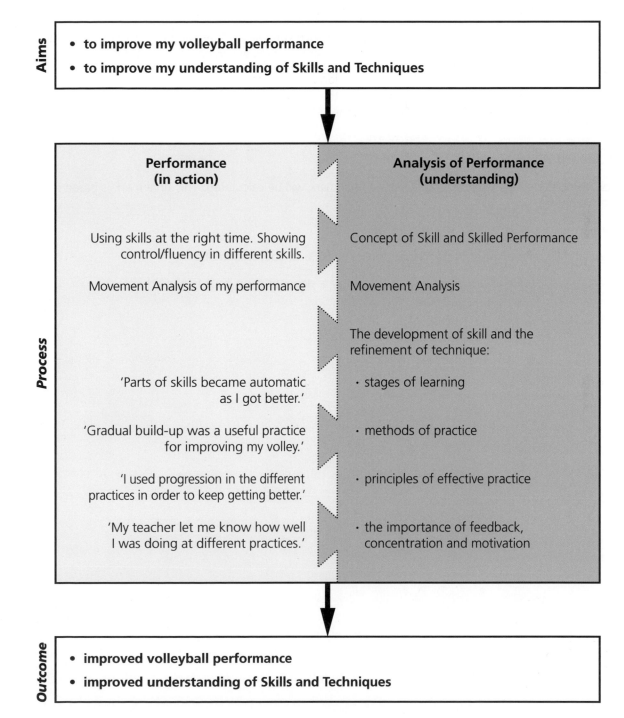

Aims

- **to improve my volleyball performance**
- **to improve my understanding of Skills and Techniques**

Process

Performance (in action)	Analysis of Performance (understanding)
Using skills at the right time. Showing control/fluency in different skills.	Concept of Skill and Skilled Performance
Movement Analysis of my performance	Movement Analysis
	The development of skill and the refinement of technique:
'Parts of skills became automatic as I got better.'	· stages of learning
'Gradual build-up was a useful practice for improving my volley.'	· methods of practice
'I used progression in the different practices in order to keep getting better.'	· principles of effective practice
'My teacher let me know how well I was doing at different practices.'	· the importance of feedback, concentration and motivation

Outcome

- **improved volleyball performance**
- **improved understanding of Skills and Techniques**

Course Assessment

To achieve a Unit you have to complete successfully the Unit Assessments. To achieve the Course award, i.e. Physical Education at Intermediate 1 Level, you have to complete successfully the Unit Assessments and the Course award Assessments.

To achieve a Unit in Analysis and Development of Performance you will be assessed in your Centre (School / College). Your teacher marks your work. The Unit Assessment involves answering questions lasting one and a half hours. Often the assessment time is split, with two sessions of 45 minutes each.

The Course Assessment is by a written examination. In the examination you need to complete three answers, each from a different area of Analysis and Development of Performance. The Intermediate 1 examination lasts one hour.

Course Award Aggregation

When you complete all the Course Assessments a final mark will be calculated. This final mark is based on the following weighting:

Performance counts as 50% of your final mark

Analysis and Development of Performance counts as 50% of your final mark.

You can achieve a Course award with an 'A', 'B' or'C' pass depending on your final mark.

SECTION 1
ACTIVITIES

Nature and purpose

Activities are different in many ways. Activities are either:

- individual or team
- directly competitive, indirectly competitive or non-competitive
- objective or subjective scoring
- indoor or outdoor

Individual or team activities

An individual activity is where you perform on your own and a team activity is where you perform with others. An example of an individual activity would be singles badminton. However, badminton could be a team activity if you are performing as part of a doubles team. Some team games have many more players; for example, football has 11 players.

Badminton singles (individual) | **Badminton doubles (team)** | **Football (team)**

Directly competitive, indirectly competitive or non-competitive activities

Some activities are competitive and some are non-competitive. Competitive activities are either directly or indirectly competitive. A directly competitive activity (rugby, football, hockey, basketball) is one where you have a direct influence on your opponent's performance. For example, you can tackle your opponent in hockey. In an indirectly competitive activity (golf, archery, trampoline) your participation is not dependent upon the performance of another performer. Non-competitive activities (hill walking) are activities where you participate for your own pleasure rather than directly or indirectly against other performers or teams.

Directly competitive (hockey) | **Indirectly competitive (golf)** | **Non-competitive (hill walking)**

Objective or subjective scoring systems

The outcome of different team and individual activities, which are either directly competitive or indirectly competitive, is decided by a variety of objective or subjective scoring methods.

Objective scoring is measured by definite means – time, points, etc. Winning by objective scoring methods includes: scoring most goals (football); runs (cricket) and points (rugby). Some activities feature a range of different objective scoring systems. For example, within athletics the time taken is used to decide running races (e.g. 100m, 200m, 400m, 800m), and height and distance measurement are used to decide jumping and throwing events (e.g. high jump, discus).

Athletics objective scoring - Time	Athletics objective scoring - Height	Athletics objective scoring - Distance

Subjective scoring methods are based on the opinions and values of those judging performances. In making scoring decisions judges need to consider many different factors. For example, in rhythmic gymnastics, the judges need to consider the range and quality of different movements and use of space and projection.

A few activities combine objective and subjective scoring methods. In ski-jumping, the final mark is based on the distance jumped (objective) and the quality of the jump (subjective).

A rhythmic gymnast performing with a ribbon

A ski jumper in flight

Indoor or outdoor activities

Activities take place either indoors or outdoors. Some activities can take place both indoors and outdoors. In football, full size games (11v11) usually take place on an outside pitch but smaller five-a-side games may well take place indoors, in a games hall. Other activities, such as badminton, usually take place indoors, but for recreational purposes are occasionally played outdoors. However, due to the influence of factors such as wind speed, competitive games always take place indoors. An exception to this is tennis, as competitive games can take place outdoors or indoors equally well provided the weather is suitable.

Study the pictures of six different activities

Diving	Gymnastics	Swimming	Basketball	Rugby	Windsurfing

For each of the activities consider: Is the activity an individual or team activity? Is the activity indirectly competitive or directly competitive? Does the activity have an objective or subjective scoring system? Compare your answers with those below.

- ▶ Diving – individual, indirectly competitive and subjective scoring
- ▶ Gymnastics - individual, indirectly competitive and subjective scoring
- ▶ Swimming - individual, indirectly competitive and objective scoring
- ▶ Basketball – team, directly competitive and objective scoring
- ▶ Rugby - team, directly competitive and objective scoring
- ▶ Windsurfing - individual, indirectly competitive and objective scoring

 For all activities in your Standard Grade course decide whether they: are individual or team activities; are directly competitive, indirectly competitive or non-competitive; have objective or subjective scoring systems; are indoor or outdoor activities.

Reasons for participating in different activities

There are many reasons why you might be more interested in some activities than others. It could be that the **physical challenge** of activities appeals to you; it could be because of the different **social benefits** that participation offers through meeting other people; it could also be that the **health benefits** of regular active participation are particularly appealing to you.

 Describe three different reasons why your favourite activity appeals to you. (One example is provided)

Activity: Basketball   Example – Access to facilities
Explanation: There is a sports centre in our town, at which we can make bookings to play basketball. Access to these facilities is at a low cost per person, and these facilities can be booked by students of our age (16). As a result, we are able to plan ahead and make bookings that suit when we want to play basketball.

Actions required in different activities

You might also be influenced in your preferences for different activities by the actions required when actively participating. Compare and contrast the different types of actions in a range of different activities.

Jumping	Kicking	Throwing	Striking	Rotating	Stretching

Creativity

Being creative is an important part of all activities and is important at all levels of performance. In most activities you require creativity in order to devise solutions to different problems.

There are many ways in which creativity can enhance performance. For example, in football the 'Cruyff turn' can help you gain an attacking advantage and wrong foot an opponent. In this turn, the attacker quickly drags the ball back, catches the defender unaware and has time to cross the ball unopposed. In many team and individual activities you are **re-creative** as a performer. Many of the moves or manoeuvres have been used before but you are using them in your own unique ways.

A footballer completing a Cruyff turn

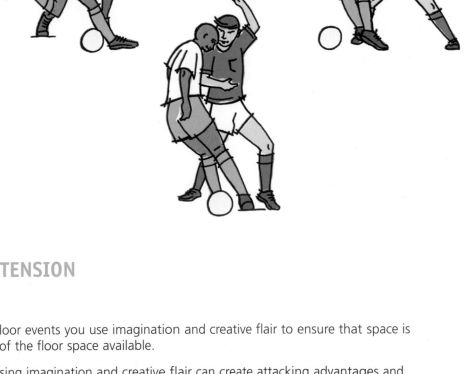

In some activities, like dance, being creative plays an important part in expressing ideas and emotions in new and original ways. Often performance is linked to accompanying music.

Different ideas and themes in dance can be expressed by a motif.

Good expressive ideas enable your performance to be interpreted easily and allow you to show different emotions and moods in your presentation. They also allow a range of movements to be improvised and developed from being creative

 ## CREDIT GRADE EXTENSION
Creativity

In indirectly competitive gymnastics floor events you use imagination and creative flair to ensure that space is used effectively by covering all parts of the floor space available.

In directly competitive team games using imagination and creative flair can create attacking advantages and create uncertainty in those who are trying to mark you.

 Study the example and add two further examples from an activity in your Standard Grade course. Explain how space was created as an attacking advantage and how space was denied as a defending advantage.

Defending example

Activity:	Role:	Creative quality:
Basketball	Guard	Double marking ball-carrier

Explanation: In basketball, if the opposing team's ball-carrier, who dribbles out of defence, is a particularly good passer my team allows the guards the option of suddenly playing two guards on the ball-carrier to try and quickly secure possession and turn defense into attack. The ball-carrier is expecting us to defend in our own half and is surprised when we disguise our intentions and suddenly double mark them further up the court.

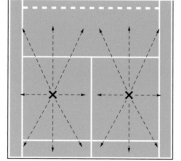

CREDIT GRADE EXTENSION
Principles of play

Applying the fundamental principles of play in team games enables you to create attacking opportunities (for example, through creating an overload) and consider how to control space in defence (for example, through applying pressure on opponents).

The fundamental principles of play in many team games involve **width and depth** in attack and defence and **delay** in defence. Evaluating your team **roles and responsibilities** and individual **strength and weaknesses** will be important in selecting tactics and planning performances which effectively apply principles of play.

Badminton example

Diagrams 1.1 and 1.2 show two different formations that are often used in badminton.

Diagram 1.1

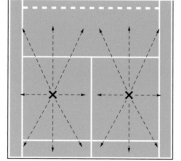

Diagram 1.2

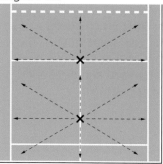

Diagram 1.1 shows a set-up which is often used when **defending**. With the players side by side in mid-court, either player can easily move forward, back or to the side to cover different shots played by the opposing team. This allows the players to cover the entire **width** of the court as well as covering its **depth** (length). In addition, **delay** is possible with this formation. Each player can adapt and respond to changes within a rally, for example, when they may move to become an attacking player.

Diagram 1.2 shows a set-up which is often used when attacking. With one player at the net and one player behind her, both players are in a strong **attacking** position. Either player can play a downward shot whether the shuttlecock comes to the front, middle or rear court. This allows the players to make full use of being in an attacking position. Each player can adapt and respond to changes within a rally when they may move from an attacking position to one of defence.

> For the different individual and team directly and indirectly competitive activities in your Standard Grade course, explain how you would evaluate your **roles and responsibilities** and individual / team **strength and weaknesses** in selecting tactics which effectively apply **principles of play** (width, depth, delay).

Tactics

A tactic is a specific way of carrying out a particular strategy and of applying in action principles of play common in games.

The choice of tactics will often depend upon the time left and the score within a game.

The overall aims of a tactic are to play to your individual and team / group strengths, and to attempt to exploit your opponent's weaknesses. Tactics can be adapted within a strategy when necessary.

Volleyball example

Using the diamond formation, different attacking and defensive tactics are possible. One such tactic is to set up some set plays within certain situations. The most common **set play** is to use all your team's three touches to try to turn a defence into an attack. The most common set of shots that teams use is first to place a soft high 'dig' shot (usually from the back of the court) to the 'setter' (who will usually be close to the net) in order to gain control of the ball and then, from this good attacking position, the setter will volley the ball to one of the two wide players who will move forward, jump high and play an attacking downward 'spike'.

Applying tactics

In all types of activities your planning is designed to highlight how your strengths and weaknesses can help performance. At times, you also should consider the strengths and weaknesses of opponents.

Badminton example

Players tend to be either **attacking** or **defensive**. Attacking players are good at hitting the shuttle downward at speed. They are looking to attack as often as possible. When their opponent hits the shuttle up they will try to get to it quickly and hit it down. Defensive players are best at playing a range of shots to different parts of the court. Their aim is to move their opponent away from the centre of the court. If their opponent has to move quickly and stretch to play different shots, the opponent is less likely to be able to return attacking downward shots. A defensive player's game plan is to keep the rallies going until he or she can make very good winning shots.

 What type of serve would you use if you were an attacking or a defensive player? This is when decision-making is important.

Service decisions

Diagram 1.3

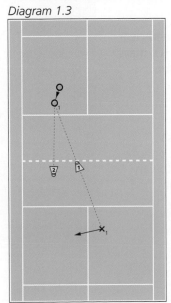

Diagram 1.4

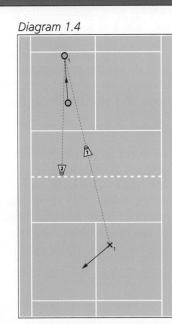

Attacking player

Your aim is to get your opponent to hit the shuttlecock up high. If they do this, you are well placed to play an attacking shot downward. A **low serve** to the front of the court is often used.

Defensive player

Your aim is to move your opponent away from the centre of the court. A **high serve** to the back of the court is often used. From here your opponent is likely to play a defensive return. You will be well placed to take control of the rally at this point.

Decisions during rallies

Attacking play example

A player who enjoys playing an attacking game will try to get to the shuttle as early as possible. They will play smashes and drop shots whenever possible. As part of their decision-making they might try to play out points in the following way:

Diagram 1.5 shows a three-shot rally. This is the type of rally an attacking player (player X in diagrams 1.5 and 1.6) would try to play. When serving, he or she would often use a low serve. His or her opponent approaches the net and tries to lift the shuttle over the attacking player. However, the attacking player will move into position quickly and play a winning smash.

Diagram 1.5

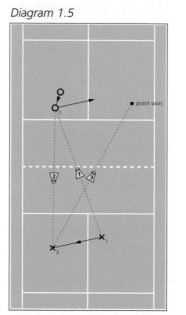

Diagram 1.6

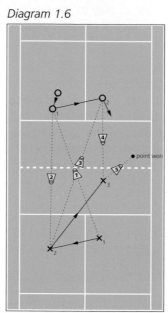

Diagram 1.6 shows one of the options that might be chosen if the smash in Diagram 1.5 was not a winning shot. The opponent manages to return the smash. However the attacking player moves quickly to the net.

 Can you decide on some of the options the attacking player may then select? One of them (shown in Diagram 4) is a drop-shot away from his or her opponent and close to the net to win the point.

Defensive play example

Defensive players are much more likely to use **building shots**. These shots are designed to keep your opponent moving around the court – to the front, back, side and so on.

Diagram 1.7 shows a rally with both players playing overhead clear shots to the back of the court. When the opposing player (O) plays a weak overhead clear which only gets to mid-court, the serving player (X) then takes advantage and plays a winning smash.

Diagram 1.7

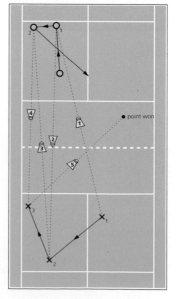

Using both attacking and defensive play

Sometimes you may find that using an attacking or defensive strategy is not working as well as you might expect. What options might you consider during the game? One such option is to vary your strategy. Why would this be done? Your opponent may find it more difficult to predict the type of shots you play. How would you vary your strategy? One way might be to **vary** the type of shots you play.

Can you work out from the examples of attacking and defensive play on pages 23-24 how you might prepare yourself to play against attacking or defensive players? What shots or combinations of shots would you play? Discuss your answers with your classmates and teacher.

 For the different individual and team directly and indirectly competitive activities in your Standard Grade course, explain how you would evaluate your **roles / positions** required for different tactics.

Personal and physical qualities in tactics

For your tactics to be effective it is important that you and other team mates have good physical and personal qualities. Physical qualities include different aspects of fitness (cardiorespiratory, muscular endurance, speed, strength, power, flexibility). Personal qualities such as determination, courage and self-confidence are also important.

Qualities		
Physical qualities	Has good strength for completing a long hit	Has good flexibility to link movements together
Personal qualities	Is confident of own skill in game	Is confident enough to perform in front of an audience

 For the different individual and team directly and indirectly competitive activities in your Standard Grade course, explain how you would evaluate your **physical and personal qualities** in different tactics.

 When performing you need to combine your physical and personal qualities in selected tactics. Study the one example below and then add two further examples from activities in which you have been actively involved.

Activity: Badminton	Role: Mixed doubles	Personal quality: Determination
Tactic: Initiating early attacks in games	Physical quality: Strength	

Explanation:
In our team, we were committed to playing to our team strengths. This involved my partner playing low serves or returns, as often as possible, to encourage the opposing team to lift the shuttle. This provided me with the chance to play a strong smash as an attempted winning point. For this tactic to work my physical quality (strength) was necessary as was our team determination. This was evident by our intention to play to our identified tactic even if there were times when this was not always successful.

Effective communication in tactics

For your tactics to be effective it is important that you and other team mates have good **verbal and non-verbal** communication skills. In basketball, for example, you need to be able to respond to spoken instruction and advice from your teacher and team mates as you change from defence to attack and back again.

At times, non-verbal signals may be more effective than verbal signals. For example, signalling (raising you arm, moving to the side, cutting and running to the basket) when being marked tightly in attack in basketball can work better than calling for the ball, as opponents will be unaware of non-verbal signals but would hear and react to verbal signals.

 For the different individual and team directly and indirectly competitive activities in your Standard Grade course, explain how you would evaluate your **communication skills** in different tactics.

CREDIT LEVEL EXTENSION
Tactics

When analysing different tactics it is important to consider whether the skills included in different tactics are effective. It could be that the decision-making associated with tactics was effective, but the skills required for completing the tactic were not. This is why you need to analyse performance before, during and after activity.

Basketball example

Diagram 1.8 shows the importance of team principles within a 4 v 4 game. In this set-up, width is created by the two forwards and depth is created by the centre. The centre moves to be on the same side of the court that the ball is on. The forwards work up and down the sidelines of the court in order to retain possession and create attacking opportunities. By moving along the top of the key the guard ensures that outlet passes can be made to and between the two forwards with little risk of a pass being intercepted.

The forwards can make cuts across the key in order to make passes to another moving player. Defenders find this more difficult to defend against than defending against a static attacker.

When applying the different options in this attacking formation there are different principles of play, attacking tactics and skills to consider.

Diagram 1.8

Principles of Play	Attacking Tactics	Effective Skills
Width	Creating attacking overload	Passing
Depth	Low risk-outlet pass	Dribbling
Delay	Passing and cutting	Shooting
	Setting screens	Effective communication

It is also possible that different aspects of **physical, skill-related and mental aspects of fitness** could affect how well different attacking tactics were applied. In the example above, speed (physical fitness) would be required in passing and cutting to the basket as would a quick reaction time (skill-related fitness) in recognising that this attacking option was available. In addition, it would be important to have mentally rehearsed (mental fitness) in advance what was going to happen when applying this tactic.

 For the different individual and team directly and indirectly competitive activities in your Standard Grade course, explain how you would evaluate your **skills** in different tactics.

 For the different individual and team directly and indirectly competitive activities in your Standard Grade course, explain how you would evaluate different aspects of **physical, skill-related and mental aspects of fitness** in different tactics.

Rules

Rules are designed to shape activities and ensure that everyone can participate on an equal basis. Rules cover: safety rules, the official and unofficial rules of fair play and specific rules for different types of activities.

Safety rules

Wearing protective equipment can help you perform safely and to the best of your ability. Study the picture below and identify the different items of safety equipment which are worn by the batsman and fielders. Compare your answers with those outlined below.

A fielder in cricket without protective equipment   *Fielders in cricket wearing protective equipment*

Batsman: Studded sole cricket boots, Gloves, Arm guard, Leg pads, Helmet

Fielders: Studded sole cricket boots and one fielder is wearing a protective helmet

Safety equipment is important, for example, when the batsman decides to play attacking rather than defensive shots.

Within the same activity players in different positions are required to wear different items of safety equipment. For example, compare the safety equipment worn by the outfield player and goalkeeper in hockey.

Two hockey players in a team – one outfield player and the goalkeeper

 For the different activities in your Standard Grade course, explain the key safety rules which are important for safe participation.

It is also important that **fixed equipment** is safely in place for different activities. For example, in throwing events in athletics (shot putt, discus and hammer), it is vital that safety netting around the throwing circle has been assembled, so that only throws in the intended direction are possible. It is also important that athletes follow the required safety rules about when to throw.

For the different activities in your Standard Grade course, explain the procedures for fixed equipment which are necessary for safe participation. (A basketball example is provided.)

Basketball: Clean dry non slippery floor; correctly attached basketball backboards and net; clear court lines; good lighting and no other equipment or people close to outside court lines. Both teams having clearly identifiable team kit is also helpful.

Awareness of safety has increased as activities have developed. For example, many more cyclists now wear safety helmets than in previous years, and this has reduced the number of head injuries.

Official and unofficial rules of fair play

All activities have official and unofficial rules of fair play. For example, consider the following rules in football.

Official rule	Offside	Explanation: Attacking players in the attacking half of the pitch must have at least one defender between them and the goalkeeper when in an active position.	Purpose of rule: The offside rule is specific to football and is designed to define where to, and how, attackers can move when in the attacking half of the pitch. The rule also provides defenders with a tactic to counter the attacking team's strengths.
Official rule	Tackling	Explanation: When challenging for possession you need to play the ball and avoid having your feet raised off the ground with studs showing.	Purpose of rule: The rule is designed to ensure safe and fair play. Winning possession by over physical challenges for the ball could injure other players and detract from the official rules about how to tackle.
Unofficial rule	Injury to opposing team player	Explanation: If an opposing team player is injured and requires medical attention it is an unofficial rule to deliberately play the ball out of the pitch. It is fair play (etiquette) for possession to be deliberately returned to the team which played the ball out of the pitch when the game restarts.	Purpose of 'rule': Safety - playing the ball out of play allows the game to be stopped and medical staff can come onto the pitch.
Unofficial rule	Shaking hands with opponents and officials	Explanation: At the end of the game it is expected that you show good etiquette and thank your opponents, whatever the result.	Purpose of 'rule': Fair play – showing that you value the game and respect others is evident by your commitment to shaking hands with opponents and officials.

For the different activities in your Standard Grade course, explain the key **official and unofficial rules** which are important for fair play.

Specific rules for different types of activities

Different activities have specific rules which have different effects on games. For example, the playing area, use of start and restart procedures and where you are able to move on court can all define activities and specific parts of activities.

Consider some of the most important specific rules and procedures which relate to taking a free throw in basketball and completing a serve in badminton.

Rule: If a player is fouled in the act of shooting the ball and misses the shot he or she is given two free throws. If a player is fouled in the act of shooting the ball and scores the basket then only one free throw is taken.

Procedure: When a free throw is awarded, the official takes the ball to the free-throw line of the offending team. After waiting for the players to take their positions, the official indicates the number of free throws awarded and gives the ball to the free thrower who must make the throw within 10 seconds.

Players' positions: Only the four marked lane spaces on each lane line may be occupied. All other players must be behind the free-throw line extended and behind the three-point field-goal line. The free thrower or any player beyond the three-point arc may not enter the free-throw lane until the ball touches the ring or backboard. However, all players who are lined up in marked lane spaces may enter the lane once the free thrower releases the ball.

Rule: To begin a point players serve and receive from the right hand service courts when the server's score is 0 or any even number of points. Players serve and receive from the left hand courts when the server's score is an uneven number of points. Both players change service courts after each point is scored.

Procedures: The server must ensure that: the racket head is no higher than the server's hand; the shuttle is contacted no higher than server's waist and that their feet are in the service court from where the service is being taken.

A serve is out if: the shuttle falls outside the service court (on the line is good), for example, if the shuttle falls into wrong service court, or short of the short service line or behind the long service line. A service (or any other shot) which hits the top of the net and continues on into the proper court is a legal hit and must be played.

Players' positions: The server may not serve unless his opponent is ready. However, the opponent is ready if a return of the service is attempted. Partners in doubles can take up any position on the courts provided they do not obstruct an opponent in any manner.

 For the different activities in your Standard Grade course, explain some of the **specific rules and procedures** which are important for effective participation.

Conduct and behaviour

Your conduct and behaviour when participating are an important part of being a 'good sportsperson'. There are general areas of good conduct and behaviour and specific conduct and behaviour issues in different team and individual activities.

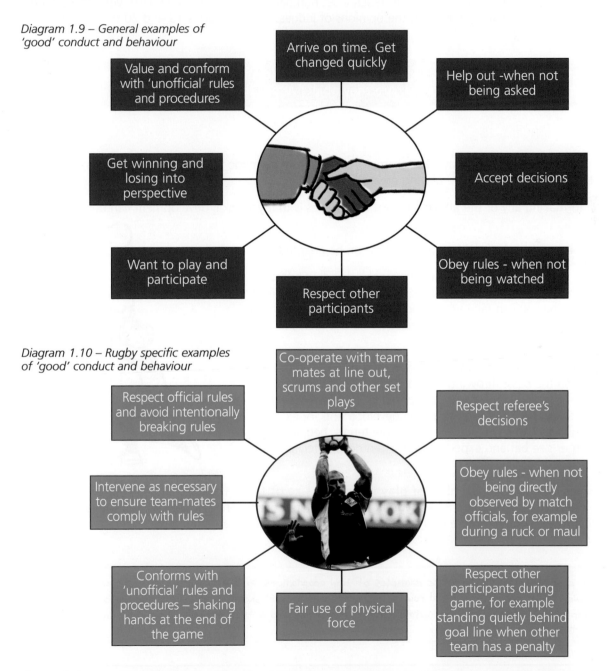

Diagram 1.9 – General examples of 'good' conduct and behaviour

- Value and conform with 'unofficial' rules and procedures
- Arrive on time. Get changed quickly
- Help out -when not being asked
- Get winning and losing into perspective
- Accept decisions
- Want to play and participate
- Respect other participants
- Obey rules - when not being watched

Diagram 1.10 – Rugby specific examples of 'good' conduct and behaviour

- Respect official rules and avoid intentionally breaking rules
- Co-operate with team mates at line out, scrums and other set plays
- Respect referee's decisions
- Intervene as necessary to ensure team-mates comply with rules
- Obey rules - when not being directly observed by match officials, for example during a ruck or maul
- Conforms with 'unofficial' rules and procedures – shaking hands at the end of the game
- Fair use of physical force
- Respect other participants during game, for example standing quietly behind goal line when other team has a penalty

If any of the good examples of conduct and behaviour are missing it will have an adverse effect on the quality of participation and possibly on the result of competition. Within the official rules of competition it is possible to penalise opponents who do not participate according to the rules.

 For the different activities in your Standard Grade course, provide some specific examples of good conduct and behaviour.

Scoring

There are many different scoring systems for different activities. Some activities have **objective scoring** systems based on results. Winning in most directly or indirectly competitive individual and team activities is decided by who has the highest score. Results can be decided by number of goals (hockey) and points (basketball). In some activities winning is decided by the first team to reach a set number of points (tennis, squash, volleyball). Other activities have **subjective scoring** based on the opinions of judges. Refer to pages 19 and 20 for further relevant details on scoring.

 For the different activities in your Standard Grade course, explain the different types of scoring systems which are used. Are they objective or subjective?

Adaptation

Activities can be adapted in many ways. For example, changes can be made to rules, equipment, duration of activity and the size and layout of the playing area.

The intention in making any of the above changes to activities is that your skill development can benefit from the changes.

Consider these examples of how different activities can be adapted.

In volleyball the official rules of full games may make skill development difficult. For this reason certain **rules** can be adapted to improve skills. For example, it might be you can take an additional touch of the ball to gain control. This might help you turn around and face the direction you wish to play the ball.

In athletics, when learning to throw the javelin you can use a lighter foam javelin to establish the basic throwing action. Similar adaptations to **equipment** are common in most racquet sports. In other activities the height of the net can be lowered to help skill development, for example in basketball or volleyball. In some activities like table tennis, beginners can learn with a larger size bat and expert players often deliberately practise using a smaller sized bat.

In many activities like rugby the **number of players** and the **size of the pitch** are reduced in order to help performance develop. Fewer players means you are likely to gain more touches of the ball and the restricted size of the pitch means you are more likely to learn that running directly at opponents is often required in order to gain distance.

 For one activity, provide three examples of how adaptations to the activity can occur. One example answer about adapting official rules is provided. Your answer should include one example of adapting equipment, one example of adapting number of players and a final example about adapting the size of the pitch.

Activity: Football	Adaptation: Changing official rules
Explanation: In football our teacher adapted the game by asking us to play passes of less than 20 metres. This meant our team had to get used to playing many short passes. This helped us improve our movement on the pitch and our ability to work better as a team.	

Small-sided games

Sometimes the normal rules of an activity can be changed in order to make some important points clearer. This is sometimes referred to as a conditioned game. For example, in basketball you may have been practising lay-up shots. It will help your performance improve if you transfer your skills from practice to actual games. An example of this would be taking lay-up shots in a game when the opportunity occurs. In order to encourage you to do this, your teacher may condition the game by altering the number of points awarded for different types of shots. A basket scored by a lay-up could be awarded 4 points instead of the usual 2. This condition helps you practise in a game setting the skills and technique which you have **developed** in practice.

Diagram 1.11

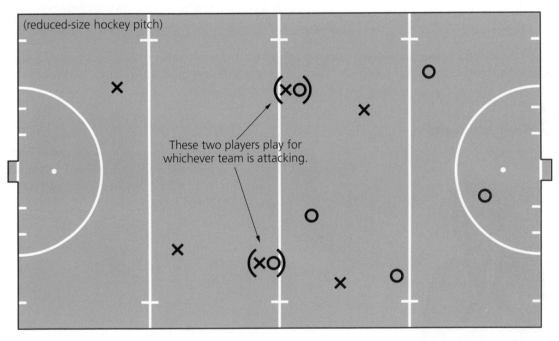

(reduced-size hockey pitch)

These two players play for whichever team is attacking.

There are other ways in which games can be adapted. For example, it is often useful to have games where there are more attackers than defenders. This will make it easier for the attackers to create scoring options. In hockey you could have four attackers versus two defenders, with attacks taking place at the one goal.

To make an adapted game more realistic you might decide to play 4 v 4 across the hockey pitch. As well as the four players in each team, you may have a further two players who play for whichever team is attacking. This effectively makes it 6 v 4 when either team is attacking; 6 v 4 will give the attackers an advantage so they will score more easily.

Once the adapted game has proved useful in improving team performance, you can continue with a small-sided game such as a 4 v 4 or 6 v 6. These games are often more useful for improving your skill level than full-size games. This is because as part of a smaller team you will get more opportunities to practise your skills than when playing as part of a larger team.

Roles and responsibilities

When **performing** as part of a group or team it is essential to understand what your individual **responsibilities** are and how your **role** relates to the roles of team mates. The success of any tactic depends on how well the team operates as a **unit**, when each player is performing **his or her own role** to the best of his or her ability.

Volleyball example

When playing in a 4 v 4 volleyball game, some players will have more defensive responsibilities, while other players have the roles of attacking rather than defending.

The individual role that you adopt in a group or team activity is dependent on many factors. These may include your physical fitness and your ability as a skilled performer, including your decision-making qualities.

Your Standard Grade course requires you to adopt a **range of different roles** in addition to being a performer. This includes helping other students; being an opponent in practice and officiating games and other competitions.

Helping other students

	Gymnastics	'I completed a feedback sheet about whether my skills were effective, limited effective or ineffective.'
	Netball	'My team mates completed a shadowing game to help improve their movement in netball. I called out the instructions and the two players had to stay on opposite sides of the circle.'

 For the different activities in your Standard Grade course, explain when you **helped other students** in your class.

Role of 'opponents' in practice

	Football	'I was the goalkeeper in this shooting practice and I made the practice realistic because I was trying to save the different shots.
	Basketball	'I provided passive defence in basketball. This allowed my opponent the attacker to practise quickly stepping past me making it easier to get the pass away.'

> For the different activities in your Standard Grade course, explain when you **adopted the role** of an opponent in practice.

Officiating games

	Volleyball	'When refereeing I had to ensure that players were ready for service to begin and to watch and see whether there were any net infringements.'
	Cricket	'When umpiring I had to judge whether to give batsman out when the bowler appealed.'

> For the different activities in your Standard Grade course, explain when you refereed or umpired games and the **major rule decisions** you were required to consider.

Personal and physical qualities

People participate in different sporting activities for various reasons. The nature and demands of each sporting activity interest people in different ways. Your own favourite sporting activities may be attractive to you in some of the ways outlined in the illustration of a small-sided hockey game shown below. This illustration shows some general performance qualities.

keeping up with play

running fast

competing with others

From this diagram, which two performance qualities are physical and which two are personal qualities?

Other demands of playing in a small-sided hockey game include:

| playing in a team | accepting decisions | having sportsmanship | using an objective scoring system | using specialist equipment |

For the different activities in your Standard Grade course, explain the different physical and personal qualities which are required for effective participation.

SECTION 2
THE BODY

Oxygen transport system

The main aim of the oxygen transport system is to help you exercise. As you increase oxygen intake during exercise (by breathing in) you can participate and train in more demanding ways. The lungs, heart, blood and muscles all play an important part in the oxygen transport system. The **respiratory** and **circulatory** systems work together to provide muscles with oxygen. This enables you to exercise.

The respiratory system enables air to be inhaled (breathed in). This allows your circulatory system to work effectively. When you breathe in, oxygen enters your lungs and is absorbed into your blood. The blood is pumped around your body by your heart. The oxygenated blood allows the cells within your body to use energy to help you exercise.

As you exercise a waste product known as carbon dioxide is produced. This is returned to the lungs by your blood as the circulatory system continues and when you breathe out the carbon dioxide leaves your body.

When you exercise your breathing is controlled automatically by your brain. You do not often have to 'think' about breathing. In some activities such as swimming you do have to 'think' about breathing as you practise; for example, when practising to improve your front crawl and breast stroke where your face is in the water for some of the time.

The circulatory system

The heart (a muscular pump) is at the centre of the circulatory system. The four chambers of the heart are mostly made up of cardiac muscle. By contracting and relaxing the heart muscles can pump blood around the body as shown in diagram 2.1.

The contractions of the heart means that blood is pumped around the body in surges which are called the pulse beat of the heart. The arteries carry blood away from the body to the vital organs and limbs (oxygenated blood) and veins return blood to the heart (deoxygenated blood).

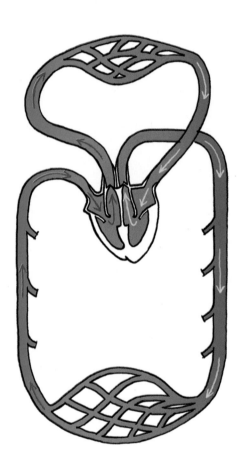

Diagram 2.1
The respiratory and circulatory system

  A simple way to check your heart rate during exercise is to pause and take your pulse for 6 seconds. Multiply your total for 6 seconds by 10 to get your heart rate per minute.

Consider with class mates which activities in your Standard Grade course will make the most demands on your oxygen transport system. Discuss the reasons for your answers.

The benefits of training

Regular exercise is very good for the heart and lungs: it increases the size of the heart. This enables more blood to be pushed around the body following a contraction of the heart muscles. This lowers the heart rate. The lower your heart rate the fitter you are. You can measure your heart rate by checking your pulse in the wrist, in the neck and often during vigorous exercise by resting the palm of your hand over your heart. A normal resting heart rate is around 50-80 beats per minute. This can increase to around 200 beats per minute. After exercise the fitter you are the faster your pulse will return to normal levels

CREDIT GRADE EXTENSION
Oxygen transport system

Different levels of oxygen intake during physical activity

The size of your lungs increases as you exercise and this provides the body with more oxygen through deeper breathing. The more oxygen you can take into your lungs the greater will be your capacity for exercise. This can be measured through breathing tests which calculate your maximal oxygen uptake or VO2 max during a minute of exercise. At rest you usually breathe about 12-15 times per minute, but this can increase to 30-40 times per minute when exercising.

Effects of lactic acid / oxygen debt

If you perform for long time intervals, for example during longer running races in athletics, orienteering or swimming, it is often difficult for your breathing to supply enough oxygen to working muscles. This leads to a build up of lactic acid in your muscles, which will eventually force you to slow down. This is because your muscles will have fatigue. Sometimes, as well, cramp can occur. Lactic acid can only be removed with oxygen. Until more oxygen arrives by deep and frequent breathing you will suffer from oxygen debt.

For these reasons it is beneficial to train regularly so that working muscles can get used to the demands of training. It is also worthwhile to try to delay the build up in lactic acid occurring. This is why in longer running races it is advisable to start at a modest pace, which you can sustain. It is also useful to have a warm down following demanding training. The warm down allows the effects of any oxygen debt to slowly disappear.

Athletics: **Longer** races, **more** chance of lactic acid build up and oxygen debt	Athletics: **Shorter** races, **less** chance of lactic acid build up and oxygen debt

Which activities in your Standard Grade course may lead to a build up of lactic acid and oxygen debt?

Body structure

The purpose of the skeleton

Your skeleton has four major functions: it supports your body; it protects vital organs (heart, lungs); blood is produced within longer bones such as the thigh (femur) and it enables movements to occur. The focus in Standard Grade PE is on movement: how do muscles, bones and joints work together?

The functions of tendon, cartilage and ligament

Muscles are attached to the bones of the skeleton by a connective tissue known as a **tendon**. When movement is necessary one end of the tendon (the origin) remains fixed while the other end (the insertion) moves. **Cartilage** acts a buffer to protect bones. There is articular cartilage at the end of bones which is hard and smooth to reduce stress. In the knee joint there are also two menisci cartilages which are softer and act as a shock absorber between the thigh and the lower leg. **Ligaments** join bones to other bones and help provide stability in joints by preventing over-stretching and over-twisting.

In diagram 2.2 and 2.3 of the knee joint below identify tendon, ligaments and different types of cartilage.

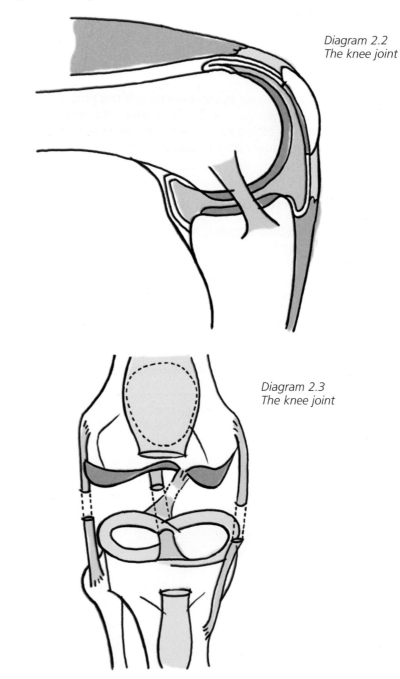

*Diagram 2.2
The knee joint*

*Diagram 2.3
The knee joint*

Muscle function and groups of muscles

Muscles function by working in pairs or groups. In diagram 2.4 of the elbow joint, as the triceps muscle relaxes and lengthens the biceps muscle contracts and shortens. This allows the elbow joint to flex. When the elbow joint is required to extend the opposite applies: the biceps muscle relaxes and lengthens and the triceps muscle contracts and shortens.

The same process applies with the knee joint. As the knee joint flexes the muscles at the front of the thigh (quadriceps) relax and lengthen while the muscles at the back of the thigh (hamstrings) contract and shorten. When the knee joint is required to extend the opposite applies: the front thigh muscles contract and shorten and the back thigh muscles relax and lengthen.

As well as enabling movement muscles are also important for good posture. If your stomach (abdominal) muscles are exercised often and have good muscle tone, this will benefit your posture. The abdominals also help with breathing and enable your back to flex and rotate.

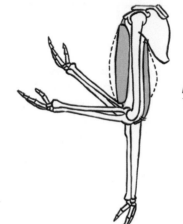

Diagram 2.4
The elbow joint

 Check your understanding of how muscles work in pairs by feeling your muscles relax and contract at elbow and knee joints.

 What are the four functions of the skeleton? What are tendons connected to?

Joints

Your skeleton is made up of bones, and **joints** are where bones meet. There are different types of joints: immovable or fixed joints such as the head (cranium); slightly moveable joints, such as the vertebrae in the spine, which are linked by cartilage and freely moveable (synovial) joints which have the greatest range of movement.

Ball and socket and hinge joints are examples of freely moveable joints. With a ball and socket joint, for example the shoulder or hip, movement is possible in all directions. With a hinge joint, for example the knee or elbow, movement is possible in one direction (plane) only in an open and close movement.

A range of movements is possible at different joints. Consider the pictures of the gymnast on the rings below. When the gymnast moves from the first balance to the second balance the arm is taken away from the centre line of the body. This is called abduction. When the gymnast moves from the second balance back to the first balance this is known as adduction, as the arm is returning towards the centre line of the body.

First balance (left) Move to second balance (middle) Return to first balance (right)

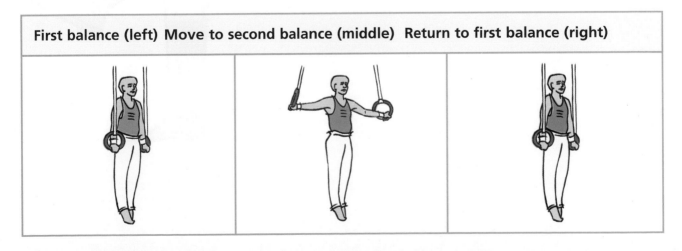

CREDIT GRADE EXTENSION
Joints

For different actions it is good if you can observe and describe the order of joint movement required in co-ordinated movements. For example, if you study the three pictures of the javelin thrower below you can see how the shoulder (ball and socket) joint leads the action (first two pictures) in establishing a strong pull position. The elbow (hinge) joint then helps keep the arm long during the throw.

Movement of a hinge joint

You can see the effect of the opening and closing effect of a hinge joint by observing and describing a kick in football. Study the picture below and note how the muscles of the upper leg and lower leg relax and contract as necessary and work together with the hinge joint to enable a powerful movement to occur. Observe also the role of the arms in providing balance.

 Can you provide other examples of the movement of a hinge joint from your Standard Grade course?

Aspects of fitness

In your Standard Grade course you will study three different aspects of fitness. These are physical, skill-related and mental aspects of fitness. Examples of each aspect of fitness are provided and many of these are specific to physical, skill-related and mental fitness. For example, rugby players require strength (a physical aspect of fitness), a sprinter in athletics requires a quick reaction time (a skill-related aspect of fitness) and a golfer will often prepare in their mind their next shot. This 'rehearsal' is a mental aspect of fitness.

It is also useful to consider the interrelated importance of the different aspects of fitness. For example, to perform a backflip in gymnastics, you require **flexibility** (an aspect of physical fitness); **co-ordination** (an aspect of skill-related fitness) and **rehearsal** (an aspect of mental fitness).

As the drive is initiated, flexibility is necessary in the back and shoulders of the gymnast. However, it is essential the drive occurs at the right time in a fluent, co-ordinated way, ensuring that the knees and hips are behind the heels as the drive begins. The co-ordination of the drive is as important as the flexibility required to perform this technique. To perform such a complex technique in a short space of time involves mentally rehearsing the series of movements that are involved. Once this has been mastered, the pattern of movements necessary can be recalled quickly from memory.

Physical fitness: cardiorespiratory endurance

Definition Cardiorespiratory endurance is the ability of the whole body to work continuously.

Introduction

When you are working to improve your cardiorespiratory endurance you need to work for long intervals at a low level of intensity. You will need a lot of oxygen to supply working muscles. This means you need to work aerobically. Long distance running and activities with similar demands such as orienteering require aerobic activity to help your cardiorespiratory endurance improve.

Anaerobic activity, by contrast, occurs when there is a shortage of oxygen. When you are working to improve your anaerobic fitness you need to work for short intervals at a high level of intensity. The 100m sprint is an anaerobic activity as there is not enough time to get oxygen to working muscles.

 Remember aerobic = with oxygen, anaerobic = without oxygen

Aerobic or anaerobic activity will lead to differences in **your pulse**, **breathing** and **body temperature**.

Aerobic activity	Pulse	Above average, 120 – 170 beats per minute
	Breathing	Above average with steady rhythm (increase from resting rate of 12 breaths a minute to 30 breaths a minute approx.)
	Body temperature	Above average, as regular exercise raises body temperature
Anaerobic activity	Pulse	From rest to high, 180–200 beats per minute in a short time
	Breathing	Little effect during exercise as exercise lasts for short time. Frequent deep breathing needed for recovery
	Body temperature	Little effect as exercise lasts for short time

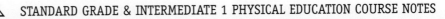

The effects of cardiorespiratory endurance on performance

In activities where you take part for relatively long periods of time, improved cardiorespiratory endurance provides you with the chance to perform better. This is because you are able to carry out skills and concentrate better if you are able to cope with the endurance demands of activities. This enables you, for example in basketball, to pass effectively throughout the game and to pay close attention to other players when defending.

When you are tired (fatigued) mistakes are more likely. This applies to games with fixed time intervals such as association football, rugby and hockey and games where the duration (the time the game lasts) is uncertain; for example, tennis, badminton and volleyball.

You can train to improve your cardiorespiratory endurance by taking part in activities, or by more general exercise activities such as cycling and jogging, or through a combination of both.

> In your Standard Grade course which skills in different team and individual activities require cardiorespiratory endurance?

Measuring cardiorespiratory endurance

Finding out about your level of cardiorespiratory endurance is a useful start point. Is it above average, average or below average? The Harvard Step Test is designed to provide you with this type of information.

Harvard Step Test

Aim To use your **recovery rate** from exercise to calculate your level of cardiorespiratory endurance

Equipment A bench to step up onto at 45cm height

Test Procedure 5 minutes at a rate of 30 step-ups onto the bench per minute

Test Calculation   Heart rate taken by pulse checks on three occasions

between 1 min and 1 min 30 s

between 2 min and 2 min 30 s

between 3 min and 3 min 30 s.

The totals from these three recordings are then used to calculate your score using the following formula:

$$\text{Score} = \frac{\text{duration of exercise in seconds}}{\text{pulse count}} \times \frac{100}{1}$$

where pulse count = (2x [heart rate after 1 minute]) +
(2 x [heart rate after 2 minutes]) + (2 x [heart rate after 3 minutes])

Use the table below to measure your performance level.

Performer	Performance level				
	High	Above average	Average	Below average	Low
Male 15/16 years	above 90	90-80	79-65	64-55	below 55
Female 15/16 years	above 86	86-76	75-61	60-50	below 50

Training to improve your cardiorespiratory endurance

Once you know whether your starting level of cardiorespiratory endurance is above average, average or below average you can consider what type of training exercises are best. Continuous, fartlek (varied pace exercise), interval and circuit training are most appropriate for improving cardiorespiratory endurance. These different methods of training are explained on pages 68 to 71.

Make sure that your training becomes more demanding as time goes on. This is called progressive overload and it is necessary to adapt this training principle to make training effective. See the examples of training methods on pages xx to xx on how this can be achieved.

CREDIT GRADE EXTENSION
Physical fitness: cardiorespiratory endurance

How to calculate your training zone

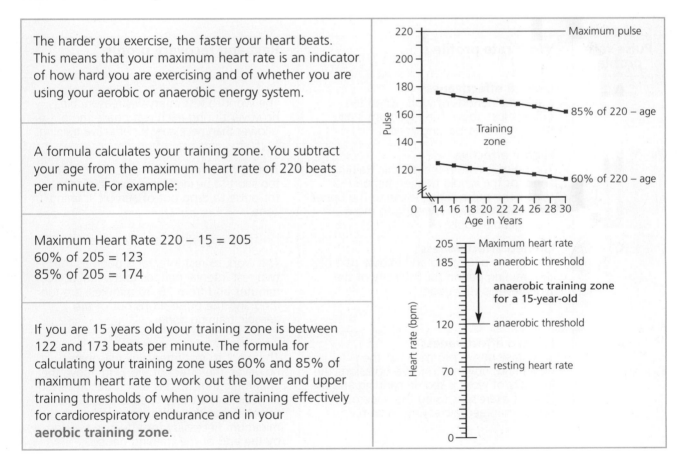

The harder you exercise, the faster your heart beats. This means that your maximum heart rate is an indicator of how hard you are exercising and of whether you are using your aerobic or anaerobic energy system.

A formula calculates your training zone. You subtract your age from the maximum heart rate of 220 beats per minute. For example:

Maximum Heart Rate 220 – 15 = 205
60% of 205 = 123
85% of 205 = 174

If you are 15 years old your training zone is between 122 and 173 beats per minute. The formula for calculating your training zone uses 60% and 85% of maximum heart rate to work out the lower and upper training thresholds of when you are training effectively for cardiorespiratory endurance and in your **aerobic training zone**.

Monitoring the effectiveness of cardiorespiratory endurance training

You can monitor your progress when exercising by checking your pulse regularly. Remember that a simple way to check your heart rate during exercise is to pause and take your pulse for 6 seconds. Multiply your total for 6 seconds by 10 to get your heart rate per minute.

Next, you need to consider the information you can learn about your cardiorespiratory endurance training from monitoring your pulse rate. This involves considering your **training zone** for aerobic exercise.

Monitoring your pulse rate during training

By measuring your pulse regularly during cardiorespiratory endurance training you can check whether your training is effective or not. Effectiveness is measured by how often the pulse is in the aerobic training zone, which is between 122 and 173 heart beats per minute. Analyse the four different pulse rates in the diagram below and consider which one represents effective training and which one indicates less effective training. Compare your analysis with the information provided about the work and rest profile of the different pulse rates.

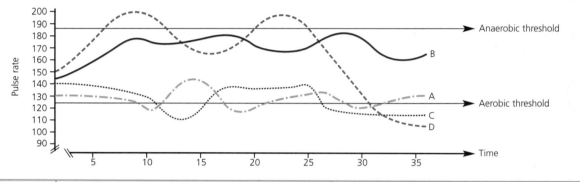

Pulse rate profile	Work rate profile	Rest and recovery profile
A	**Limited effectiveness** Has three periods of work when the pulse is just above the minimum limit for the aerobic training zone.	The work to rest interval is reasonable, however during each rest phase the pulse is lower than necessary for effective training.
B	**Highly effective** The pulse is within the aerobic training zone for the whole training period (30 mins.) The pulse comes close to the upper limit before slowly lowering to more manageable levels.	The work to rest interval excellent, not too short to be ineffective, not too long for pulse to drop out of aerobic training zone.
C	**Limited effectiveness** During the beginning and middle part of the training period the intensity of the work level is very good.	The work to rest interval is poor, as the two rest interval periods (between 12-15 minutes and from 26-30 minutes) are too long and the pulse drops out of the aerobic training zone.
D	**Limited effectiveness** The pulse rate is promising at the beginning, however on two occasions the intensity of work is too demanding and the level of exercise is using the anaerobic rather than aerobic energy system.	The work to rest interval is reasonable, however, the effect of working above the anaerobic threshold is that it becomes too difficult for recovery to take place. The effect is that the pulse drops below the minimum necessary for effective training by the end of the training period.

Training to develop anaerobic endurance

Anaerobic exercise puts a greater stress on your circulatory and respiratory systems. For these reasons you need to be aerobically fit before beginning anaerobic endurance training. Interval training which is based on very high effort followed by lighter effort or rest would work best. The lighter effort or rest phase would enable your body to remove lactic acid and reduce your oxygen debt.

 For different activities in your Standard Grade course, explain the possible performance benefits of having improved cardiorespiratory endurance.

Physical fitness: muscular endurance

Definition: Muscular endurance is the ability of muscles to work continuously.

Introduction

Using the same muscle groups repeatedly over long periods of time requires muscular endurance. To improve your muscular endurance you need to work muscle groups for long intervals at a relatively low level of intensity. Rowing and cycling are activities where the demands are more on specific muscles groups than the cardiorespiratory system. Poor muscular endurance leads to fatigue and your muscles will feel tired and heavy.

The effects of muscular endurance on performance

For many activities you require good muscle tone in major muscle groups for effective performance. For example, in badminton you require good muscular endurance to be able to move forward to the net to play shots as well as to reach up and play overhead shots repeatedly during games. If your muscles become fatigued you will move more slowly. This will mean that you arrive late to play shots and do not complete shots as well as when you are not tired.

1 A badminton player moving forward to the net to play shuttlecock

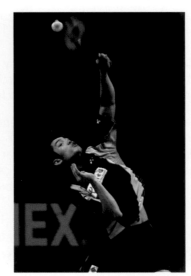

2 A badminton player jumping and reaching to play an overhead shot

In your Standard Grade course, which skills in different team and individual activities require muscular endurance?

Measuring muscular endurance

There are various tests for measuring muscular endurance. The Bent Knee Sit-Up Test is an effective test for measuring the muscular endurance of the abdominal (stomach) muscles. The test procedure is as follows:

1 Start lying on the floor, hands behind your head, knees bent with feet flat on floor

2 Your partner holds your feet down

3 Sit-up using your abdominal muscles until your elbows are passed your knees. Then lower yourself down again. This is one sit-up.

4 Do as many sit-ups as you can in 30 seconds. Your partner records the time and the number of successful sit-ups completed.

Training to improve your muscular endurance

Overloading muscles in training will provide more oxygen for muscle groups and, over time, your ability for muscles to cope with greater work in different activities will improve.

Circuit training is an effective way of improving muscular endurance. A circuit would typically include the following types of exercises: sit-ups; burpees; press-ups; step-ups; shuttle runs and dips.

1 sit-ups 2 burpees 3 press-ups
4 step-ups 5 shuttle run 6 dips

Each of the exercises involved in the circuit is particularly useful for different muscle groups. In the circuit it is important to ensure that the same muscles are not exercised in successive exercises. For this reason the press-ups and the dips which mostly involve upper body muscles are kept apart.

Other forms of training are also possible for muscular endurance, such as weight training and muscular endurance training when practising activity specific skills at the same time. For weight training, exercises would involve low weights and high repetitions as the muscular work is endurance based. For training involving skills practice at the same time, it is important that the skills can be relatively easily performed so that endurance work can continue with few interruptions due to skills breaking down.

CREDIT GRADE EXTENSION
Physical fitness: muscular endurance

Monitoring the effectiveness of muscular endurance training

When training, it is useful to measure your initial level of muscular endurance in different exercises when taking part in different activities. This enables you to set challenging but achievable targets through comparing your performance against how you performed at the outset. It also enables you to calculate how best to progressively overload your training, for example by completing more exercises.

Progressive overload for muscular endurance would usually involve completing exercises for longer periods of time (duration) or more repetitions of exercises (frequency). You are less likely to add intensity to exercises as the work is based on endurance. So, for example, when weight training you might complete exercises for longer periods of time or complete more repetitions of exercises but not exercise using heavier weights (intensity).

For one activity in your Standard Grade course, explain how you could add to the duration or frequency of exercises in a weight training programme.

For one activity in your Standard Grade course, explain how you could add to the duration or frequency of exercises when you are practising activity specific skills at the same time.

The effects of increased muscular endurance on the body

There are many performance benefits of muscular endurance. Some of these benefits will be specific to different activities, but in general improved muscular endurance should ensure that you have better muscle tone and posture. This often means that you are able to complete skills more effectively (improved control and fluency), especially when you begin to get tired.

 For different activities in your Standard Grade course, explain the possible performance benefits of having improved muscular endurance.

Physical fitness: strength

Definition Strength is the maximum amount of force a muscle, or group of muscles, can exert in a single effort.

Introduction

The three main types of strength are: static; explosive and dynamic. Different activities require different types of strength. To improve your strength you need to work muscle groups for short intervals at a relatively high level of intensity.

The effects of strength on performance

For effective performance forwards in rugby try in certain scrums to hold the scrum steady. They are trying to use their static strength to prevent the other team's forwards from driving them backwards. Explosive strength is used in single actions when maximum energy is needed. Many throwing and jumping events in athletics (such as long jump and javelin) require explosive strength. Dynamic strength is needed in swimming short distances that take up to approximately two minutes. For example, in a 100 m front crawl race, a swimmer continuously works the major muscles of the arm and shoulder to gain propulsion.

Static strength

Explosive strength

Dynamic strength

 In your Standard Grade course, which skills in different team and individual activities require strength?

Measuring strength

There are various tests for measuring static, explosive and dynamic strength. A grip dynamometer is used to measure **static strength** in the hand and forearm. You squeeze as hard as possible for a few seconds. You can compare your strength in your right and left forearm.

A standing long jump test is often used to measure **explosive strength**. You complete a two-footed jump and measure the distance from the marked start line to the back of your furthest back foot on landing.

For **dynamic strength** various exercises such as sprint starts, squat thrusts and press-ups are often used. These exercises are similar to those used for measuring muscular endurance. For measuring dynamic strength the exercises would usually last for a shorter training time.

Training to improve your strength

Weight training is an effective way to improve all types of strength. Exercises will vary according to the type of strength requiring improvement (static, explosive and dynamic).

When completing a weight training programme you need to consider how many **repetitions** and **sets** of different exercises you will complete. For example, if you might complete 10 repetitions of an exercise on 3 occasions in a set.

 Take care to ensure that you avoid placing any unnecessary strain on your muscles when weight training. Any increases in weight should be gradual.

- Moving a heavy weight a few times increases static strength
- Moving a medium weight very fast improves explosive strength
- Moving a light weight improves dynamic strength initially (and muscular endurance if continued for a longer time)

Weight training can be completed using barbells (a long bar with weights attached) and dumbbells (a short bar with weights attached). This is referred to as using free-standing weights and it is often useful for a partner to help as a supporter.

Free-standing weights exercises

Many schools also have various types of weight training machines in fitness suites where similar weight training exercises can be completed.

A weight training room

 For one activity in your Standard Grade course, explain the number of repetitions and sets you would use for different exercises in a weight training programme.

CREDIT GRADE EXTENSION
Physical fitness: strength

Monitoring the effectiveness of strength training

As with other aspects of physical fitness, it is useful to measure your initial level of strength in different exercises when taking part in different activities. For strength training it is also beneficial to ensure the type of muscle action (isometric, isokinetic and isotonic) links to the muscle group being exercised and to the weight training methods being used.

Isometric exercises are used when muscles are required to be stable and still. This would be useful in gymnastics, for example, when strength is required for balances.

A gymnast using their strong arm, stomach and leg muscles to retain balance

Isokinetic exercises are used when muscles require control through a range of movements. During these types of exercise the amount of muscular force exerted will increase and decrease as movement occurs; for example, in football the rapid extension of the lower leg during the kicking motion is necessary. Isokinetic exercises which challenge the quadriceps (front thigh) muscles to contract maximally and at a high speed can improve the strength of the kicking action. Such exercises can be practised using either free-standing weights or on different machines in a weights room (fitness suite).

Isotonic exercises involve the same weight but the muscles involved either shorten or lengthen as necessary. The 'two hands curl' in the free-standing weights exercise diagram above is an example of an isotonic exercise as the elbow joint flexes and extends.

Progressive overload for strength would usually involve more repetitions of exercises (frequency) and adding to the intensity of exercises by increasing the weights involved.

 For one activity in your Standard Grade course, explain how you could add to the frequency or intensity of exercises in a weight training programme.

The effects of increased strength on the body

There are many performance benefits of strength. Some of these benefits will be specific to different activities, but in general improved strength should ensure that you have the capacity to complete actions which require strength and co-ordination; for example, hitting a long pass in hockey.

A hockey player preparing to hit a long pass

For different activities in your Standard Grade course, explain the possible performance benefits of having improved strength.

Physical fitness: speed

Definition Speed is the ability to cover a distance or perform a movement in a short time.

Introduction

Most activities require speed in some way. To improve your speed you need to work muscle groups for short intervals at a relatively high level of intensity.

The effects of speed on performance

In many team and individual activities speed is required by the whole body; on other occasions only part of the body is required.

Team activity Whole body	Individual activity Whole body	Team activity Part of body	Individual activity Part of body
Wingers in football need speed to get free from defenders	The gymnast needs speed in the run up and take-off to gain flight onto the horse (box)	In badminton doubles players need speed to get to the net quickly to return shots at the net	The table tennis player requires to bring his arm forward quickly when playing a forehand smash

Speed is a mix of physical fitness and also technique. For example, to run quickly you need strong muscles as well as a good stride pattern and running style.

In your Standard Grade course which skills in different team and individual activities require speed? Identify whether it is the whole body or part of the body which requires speed in each example you choose.

Measuring speed

There are various tests for measuring speed. Many of these involve sprinting and are relatively easy to measure with a stop watch. Most sprints tend to be over relatively short distances such as 10m and 20m. In many activities, such as football or hockey, these are the distances you would be expected to sprint during a game when trying to close down attackers. For this reason many sprint running tests might also involve changes in direction. This means that test results will link closely to specific speed needs in different games.

Training to improve your speed

Speed is best improved by increasing strength in the main muscles required for different activities. When training to improve speed you will be using anaerobic (without oxygen) energy most. For this reason you need to ensure that your rest and recovery time is long enough. This often means that you would work for 1 repetition of an exercise and rest for 4 times as long. For example, sprinting for 5 seconds and resting for 20 seconds, and so on.

CREDIT GRADE EXTENSION
Physical fitness: speed

Monitoring the effectiveness of speed training

When training, it is useful to measure your initial level of speed in different exercises and when taking part in different activities. Progressive overload for speed would usually involve completing exercises for short periods of time (duration) with repetitions of exercises (frequency) following adequate time for rest and recovery. Rest is necessary as it allows time for the reduction of oxygen debt and the removal of lactic acid.

When working on your speed fitness, it is useful for you to recognise that certain inherited factors (such as the number of fast twitch muscle fibres) and other factors (such as your body shape), will affect improvement.

Take care to ensure that you avoid placing any unnecessary strain on your heart and lungs when training your anaerobic energy system. Begin with aerobic exercise and transfer to anaerobic exercise when ready.

For one activity in your Standard Grade course, explain how you could add to the intensity of exercises in a speed training programme.

For one activity in your Standard Grade course, explain how you could add to the intensity of exercises when you are practising to improve activity specific skills and speed at the same time.

The effects of increased speed on the body

There are many performance benefits of improved speed. Some of these benefits will be specific to different activities, but in general improved speed should ensure you have the capacity to complete actions which require speed and agility, for example the volleyball player completing a dig shot has to move quickly and precisely to play the shot.

A volleyball player getting low and behind the ball to play a dig shot

For different activities in your Standard Grade course, explain the possible performance benefits of having improved speed.

Physical fitness: power

Definition Power is the combination of **strength** and **speed**.

Introduction

Power is very important in explosive events; for example, in jumping and throwing events in athletics, where you need both speed and strength. Power can only last for a few seconds. To improve your power you need to work muscle groups for short intervals at a high level of intensity.

The effects of power on performance

In many activities power is required; for example, in the long jump and shot putt in athletics. It is also needed, along with effective technique, in different kicking and striking actions; for example, kicking for distance in rugby and batting in softball.

The shot putter uses speed and strength to travel across the circle and putt the shot

The long jumper uses speed and strength at take-off to jump at long distance.

In your Standard Grade course which skills in different team and individual activities require power?

Measuring power

There are various tests for measuring power. In the standing high jump or standing long jump tests explosive power is needed as you are trying to jump as high or as far as possible from a standing start. In both of these tests explosive power is created by powerful leg muscles and by gaining additional height or distance by swinging your arms.

Vertical Jump Test

Stretch you arms above your head and mark the height with your fingertips. Then stand sideways to the marking board and jump as high as possible and mark the height with your fingertips. Measure the distance between the two marks.

Standing Long Jump

From behind the take-off line, complete a two-footed jump and measure the distance from the take-off line to the rearmost mark of your landing.

Training to improve power

Explosive power is best improved by increasing strength in the main muscles used for different activities and by completing exercises requiring speed. If you are using weight training to improve strength, ensure you take into account your own weight when calculating training values.

CREDIT GRADE EXTENSION
Physical fitness: power

Monitoring the effectiveness of power training

When you monitor power you have to consider the size of the force applied as well as the speed of the force applied. In the shot putt example used earlier, the best thrower is the athlete who can apply the largest force at the quickest speed. Power, in this example, is shown by the rate of change of work in a short time interval.

To replicate the demands of power as needed in various activities adding progressive overload would usually involve completing exercises for very short periods of time (duration) as part of a few repetitions of exercises (frequency), followed by adequate time for rest and recovery. As your training progresses, you would add to the intensity of exercises by increasing weight if weight training. By doing this you would be adding to the **resistance** involved in completing exercises. For speed-related work decreasing rest times would be suitable as a method of increasing the intensity of exercises.

 For one activity in your Standard Grade course, explain how you could add to the intensity of exercises in a power based training programme.

For one activity in your Standard Grade course, explain how you could add to the intensity of exercises when you are practising to improve activity specific skills and speed at the same time.

The effects of increased power on the body

There are many performance benefits of improved power. Some of these benefits will be specific to different activities, but in general improved power should ensure you have the capacity to complete actions which require explosive power and co-ordination; for example, in throwing the javelin.

For different activities in your Standard Grade course, explain the possible performance benefits of having improved power.

Physical fitness: flexibility

Definition Flexibility is the **range of movement** across a joint.

Introduction

Most activities require flexibility. Having good flexibility reduces the chances of you straining or pulling muscles. Controlled stretching exercises can be used to maintain and improve flexibility, which is often referred to as either suppleness or mobility.

The effects of flexibility on performance

In many activities flexibility is required; for example, when hurdling in athletics and when swimming back crawl. The hurdler needs hip flexibility in particular, as this will help the hurdler clear the hurdles with minimum effort and maximum efficiency.

The swimmer needs back flexibility to help when pushing off, and arm and shoulder flexibility to produce a wide range of movement. This will help make the swimming stroke more effective.

To improve flexibility you stretch and move joints just beyond the point at which you feel resistance. Flexibility is affected by the type of joint and muscle attachment. Flexibility is limited by ligaments which hold joints in place. The elasticity of tendons which attach muscles to bones and joints also limits the degree of flexibility possible.

There are two types of flexibility: static and dynamic flexibility. Static flexibility is necessary when you are holding a balance in gymnastics.

A gymnast on the beam who has very good static hip and leg flexibility

Dynamic flexibility requires flexibility for a short time within your overall performance. For example, the high jumper requires dynamic flexibility when arching their back as part of their overall high jump attempt.

A high jumper with very good dynamic flexibility in their back

In your Standard Grade course, which skills in different team and individual activities require flexibility? For each example identified, decide whether it is static or dynamic flexibility which is required.

Identify a flexibility exercise which could develop flexibility in the following joints – neck, shoulder, elbow, hips, knee and ankle.

Measuring flexibility

There are various tests for measuring flexibility. Two examples are highlighted here, the first the 'sit-and-reach test' measures the flexibility at the hip joint and in the muscles at the back of the thigh (hamstrings).

For this test after a warm up you sit on the floor and with legs extended and feet flexed you stretch forward with both hands as far as possible. You record how far beyond your toes you can stretch. It is important that you stretch forward carefully and not in a sudden way. You can compare your results with the figures for your age group. For example:

Age 15 – 16 years	High score	Above average	Average	Below average	Low score
Male	Above 14 cm	13-11 cm	10-7 cm	6-4 cm	Less 4 cm
Female	Above 15 cm	14-12 cm	11-7 cm	6-4 cm	Less 4 cm

As you can see, females are usually more flexible than males.

The second example, the 'trunk extension test' measures the flexibility of the lower back. In this test you lie face down on the floor with your hands behind your head. The idea is to measure how high you can lift your chin off the floor. Your feet have to remain on the floor as you complete this test.

Training to improve flexibility

Exercises to maintain and improve flexibility are usually either **static** or **active** exercises. In static exercises you hold a stretched position for a few seconds.

Here are two examples of static stretching

With active (ballistic) stretching exercises you use movement to move a body part at a joint. You should warm up carefully before completing active stretching exercises such as the 'side stretch' pictured below.

Here is an example of active stretching

CREDIT GRADE EXTENSION
Physical fitness: flexibility

Monitoring the effectiveness of flexibility training

Many of the potential benefits of effective flexibility training are described on page 56 and page 57. Maintaining and improving your flexibility provides you with the opportunity to perform as skilfully as possible. For this reason, you can monitor your flexibility by analysing it as part of your game analysis as well as by completing flexibility tests if you wish.

 For one activity in your Standard Grade course, explain how you could increase intensity of flexibility exercises in a training programme.

 For one activity in your Standard Grade course, explain how you could add to the intensity of exercises when you are practising to improve activity specific skills and flexibility at the same time.

The effects of increased flexibility on the body

Improved flexibility should ensure you have the capacity to complete actions which require flexibility as well as other physical fitness and skill-related fitness qualities. For example, among other qualities, the skier pictured below requires flexibility, dynamic strength and agility.

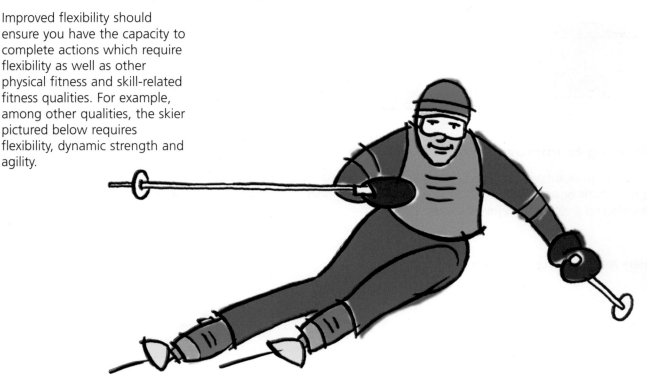

A slalom skier in action who shows very good flexibility, dynamic strength and agility

 For different activities in your Standard Grade course, explain the possible performance benefits of having improved flexibility.

Skill-related fitness: co-ordination

Co-ordination is the ability to control movements smoothly and fluently. To perform in a co-ordinated way, groups of muscles work in a specific sequence to create effective movements. For example, you need strong arm, shoulder, abdominal and back muscles to throw the javelin. However, in addition to explosive power you require co-ordination so that your explosive power is used at the correct stage of the throw and to its maximum potential. For difficult skills with complex co-ordination requirements, specific practices are required.

 In your Standard Grade course which skills in different team and individual activities require co-ordination?

 CREDIT GRADE EXTENSION
Skill-related fitness: co-ordination

As your co-ordination improves you are able to move your joints and muscles in the correct order. This leads to improvements in your hand and eye co-ordination, for example when catching a ball.

Improved co-ordination also improves control and fluency. This is important in events such as the triple jump in athletics where co-ordinated movements enable speed to be carried through to the final jump phase. This requires co-ordinated body movements in each phase of the jump. From the picture below identify how the triple jumper uses the arms and legs to achieve rhythm and fluency. Effective co-ordination should ensure that there is no jerkiness when performing a triple jump.

The key stages involved in the triple jump from take-off to landing

For different activities in your Standard Grade course, explain the possible performance benefits of having improved co-ordination.

Skill-related fitness: agility

Agility is the ability to move the body quickly and precisely. When completing a dig shot in volleyball, you need to be able to move quickly, lower your centre of gravity and get behind the ball in order to maintain control of the shot. In volleyball, agility requires both flexibility and speed.

In most activities it is an advantage to be agile; for example, when avoiding being tackled in rugby, dribbling at speed in hockey or reaching for a low net shot in badminton.

An agile badminton player stretching to return a shot in badminton

 In your Standard Grade course, which skills in different team and individual activities require agility?

 CREDIT GRADE EXTENSION
Skill-related fitness: agility

As your agility improves you are likely to make quick changes in direction; for example, through diving to save a shot in football. Improved agility will help you react quickly in ways which are often unexpected. For example, an attacker in football can disguise the direction in which they are going to shoot. This reduces the time available for the goalkeeper to react and increases the need for them to be agile.

An agile goalkeeper reacting quickly to save a shot in football

 For different activities in your Standard Grade course, explain the possible performance benefits of having improved agility.

Skill-related fitness: balance

Balance is the ability to retain the centre of gravity over your base of support. Balancing requires the control of different groups of muscles. The exact muscle requirements depend upon the nature of the task. Static balances such as a headstand in gymnastics require you to hold a balance, while dynamic balances require you to maintain balance under constantly changing conditions.

Static balance   **Dynamic balance**

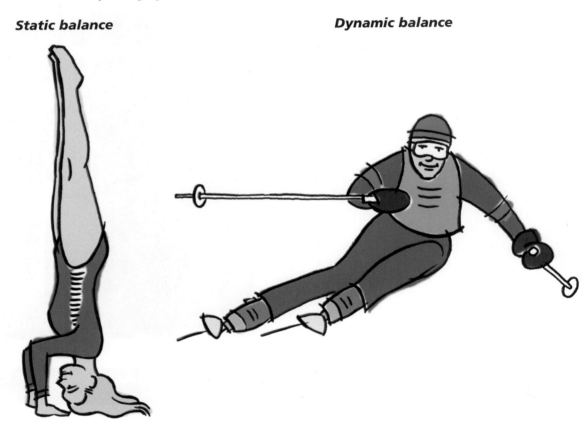

 For the activities in your Standard Grade course which skills in different team and individual activities require balance?

 CREDIT GRADE EXTENSION
Skill-related fitness: balance

As your static balance improves you are more likely to be able to show fine motor control and good control of your strength and body weight. In the headstand balance you move from using large body movements to complete the balance using fine body movements which help improve your stability.

As your dynamic balance improves you are more likely to be able to show control in demanding situations; for example, when skiing you can constantly adjust your dynamic balance as you travel over changing terrain in order to remain in balance.

 For different activities in your Standard Grade course, explain the possible performance benefits of having improved static and dynamic balances.

2 THE BODY
ASPECTS OF FITNESS

Skill-related fitness: reaction time

Reaction time is the time taken between the recognition of a signal and the start of the movement. It is linked to speed. If you are playing as a guard in basketball you might need to respond quickly. A fast reaction time when marking the attacker, and quick court movements, would assist in effective performance. This would help when the attacker decides to pass, dribble or shoot.

A defender in basketball reacting quickly in order to defend effectively

In your Standard Grade course, which skills in different team and individual activities require a fast reaction time?

CREDIT GRADE EXTENSION
Skill-related fitness: reaction time

As your reaction time improves you are likely to think and respond more quickly. This should lead to fewer errors in movement and more time to make decisions. For example, in a line out in rugby union, practice between the thrower and the jumpers and supporters should ensure that you are able to secure possession. This will be more difficult to achieve when the opposing team have the throw in, as you will have less time to respond and time your jump accordingly.

A line-out in rugby union

For different activities in your Standard Grade course, explain the possible performance benefits of having improved reaction time.

Mental-related fitness

Mental preparation is important in many activities; for example, in long-distance running events, such as the 1500m. It is a good idea to think ahead to how you are going to cope with tiredness when running a 1500m race. You can mentally prepare in a positive way by breaking the whole race down into a series of smaller steps. Then, as you achieve the smaller steps, such as 'coping with the opening lap' (for example, runner X below is quite content that she is in third place in lap 1) and 'keeping up with the leaders in the middle laps of the race', you feel good about your performance and can keep going to the finish in a fast time. By mentally preparing ahead like this you are better placed to do well.

Your mental preparation is based on **concentration** (watching other runners closely during the race and remembering individual lap times), **confidence** (you are comfortable running behind the leader during opening and middle parts of the race) and your **motivation** (desire to win).

Lap 1 *Laps 2-3* *Lap 4*

 In your Standard Grade course, which skills in different team and individual activities would benefit from mental preparation?

 ## CREDIT GRADE EXTENSION
Mental-related fitness

Your mental preparation is likely to be high if you feel safe about what you are doing. This is especially the case in some activities like gymnastics when you are practising new and often complex skills for the first time. Ensuring that there are adequate safety mats in place and often a class mate to support your movements, as necessary, can help improve your confidence and overall mental preparation.

In the picture below the extensive number of support mats and the close observation by the teacher provides reassurance when practising gymnastics skills on the beam.

Young gymnasts training on the beam

 For different activities in your Standard Grade course, explain the possible performance benefits of safe equipment and support.

Warm up

The aim of an effective warm up is to gradually get your whole body prepared for work.

Four key stages are often involved in an effective warm up. These are:

1	Increase your pulse rate by raising the blood flow to the muscles. This can be achieved through aerobic exercise such as jogging, building up to light running for a few minutes. After this exercise you should have raised your body temperature and increased joint mobility.	
2	Complete stretching exercises of the large muscle groups. See notes on flexibility on pages 56 and 57 for advice on completing static and dynamic stretching exercises. Stretching exercises should last a further few minutes. After this exercise your muscles should be supple.	
3	Refresh a few specific skill-related practices for the activity you are participating in. For example, if the activity is basketball practice a few lay up shots for a further few minutes. After this exercise you should be familiar with some of the performance skills involved in the activity.	
4	Prepare your mind for the activity ahead. You might wish to note these down. After this exercise you should be able to focus on your performance improvement objectives.	

 Take care to ensure that you avoid placing any unnecessary strain on your muscles, joints and tendons when warming up.

Describe for the activities in your Standard Grade course how you would complete an effective warm up.

Warm down

The warm down (or cool down) is an equally necessary part of your activity training routine. The purpose of the warm down is to help your body to recover after exercise.

It should start with jogging or light running. This will help the blood circulation to carry more oxygen to the muscles, which in turn will help reduce muscle stiffness as lactic acid is removed quicker. This exercise should last a few minutes. Complete your warm down with some stretching. This will help keep muscles supple.

 Describe for the activities in your Standard Grade course how you would complete an effective warm down.

Principles of training

For a physical fitness training programme to be effective you need to apply the training principles of specificity and progressive overload to your programme. This can be achieved by adapting duration, intensity and frequency in your programme.

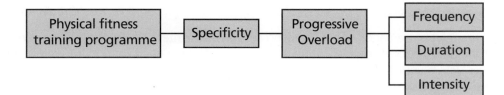

Specificity is the first key principle in training. Specificity is crucial to physical fitness performance improvement. Training has to be specific to your needs; it has to be relevant to the activity, and to your existing levels of fitness and ability.

For example, if you were a basketball player completing a physical fitness training programme you would need to ensure that training was specific to your role within a basketball team (forward, centre, guard), relevant to basketball and to your existing ability and physical fitness levels.

If you were a hockey player who needed speed for short sprints in a game you might complete some shuttle sprints in training to develop speed.

 For one activity in your Standard Grade course, describe how you could ensure physical fitness training was specific to your needs

Progressive overload is the second key principle in training. Progressive overload is crucial to performance improvement and occurs when you exercise at increasingly greater levels: you progressively add to the demands of your physical fitness programme as your body adjusts to the benefits of your current fitness programme.

For example, if you are an athlete training for the 1500m, you could set time targets for different parts of your training programme. Once you have achieved these time targets, you could create new time targets to ensure progressive overload is included in your training. If you are a basketball player taking part in a strength training programme to improve your thigh strength, progressively increasing the weights is one way of ensuring that progressive overload is built into your programme.

The progressive overload principle can be **adapted** by varying the **frequency**, the **intensity** and the **duration** of your training.

Frequency refers to the regularity and routine of your training sessions. How often you train varies according to the demands of the activity. Some activities require many training sessions per week over a number of months before improvements occur. For the average performer to improve cardiorespiratory endurance, he or she would need to exercise with his or her heart rate within the training zone for 20 to 30 minutes for three to four sessions per week over two to three months. However, if you are an elite performer training for competitive long distance swimming races, you would swim much more often per week. If you are a young performer in the early stages of playing full games of hockey, fitness improvements would require less training.

Intensity refers to the relative demands of your training sessions. The intensity of your training varies according to the demands of the activity. For cardiorespiratory endurance work, you need to monitor your heart rate to ensure that you work within your training zone. This may be achieved by running at about 50-60% of your full speed. For sprint work involving anaerobic fitness, you need to train at a high level of intensity for shorter periods. This will mostly involve you running at about 80%-90% of your full speed. The setting of the levels of intensity is very important, especially for the speed / strength / power training aspects of physical fitness.

Athlete	Aspect of fitness	Percentage effort	Training Session
Long distance runner	Cardiorespiratory endurance	50–60% (lower intensity level)	Longer, more continuous work with some small rests
Sprinter	Speed	80–90% (higher intensity level)	Shorter, with times of very hard work and some quite long rests to recover

Intensity can also be adapted by adjusting the work / rest interval. For example, in a cardiorespiratory endurance programme, progressively reducing the rest intervals throughout the programme adds to the intensity of the workload (even if the actual demands of the exercises remain the same).

First session, swim 4 x 25m lengths @ 60% maximum speed. Rest for **60** seconds. Repeat twice.
Next session, swim 4 x 25m lengths @ 60% maximum speed. Rest for **50** seconds. Repeat twice.
Next session, swim 4 x 25m lengths @ 60% maximum speed. Rest for **40** seconds. Repeat twice.
Next session, swim 4 x 25m lengths @ 60% maximum speed. Rest for **30** seconds. Repeat twice.

Duration refers to the length of planned time spent training. The duration of your training varies according to the demands of the activity. Within the context of a training programme short, intensive training sessions promote anaerobic fitness improvement; longer, moderately intensive sessions develop aerobic endurance.

Anaerobic fitness improvements are most likely to occur after six to eight weeks, provided the intensity of training work is high (80%-90% of your maximum intensity). Aerobic endurance improvements are most likely to occur after two to three months if the frequency of training is three to four times per week. Duration also applies to the length of individual training sessions within a training programme (e.g. 60 minutes at the beginning rising to 80 minutes by the end of the training programme).

For the activity chosen previously (when considering specificity), describe how you add progressive overload to you specific training needs.

CREDIT GRADE EXTENSION
Principles of training

The dangers of over training

With any training programme it is important that you do not over train. This can be avoided by taking an adequate **rest and recovery** time during training sessions and by **avoiding over training** each week.

For example, a swimmer who specialised in sprint events could complete a 50m sprint and then rest for 30 seconds, before completing two further 50m sprints with a further 30 seconds rest and recovery each time after each sprint. Following this 'set' it would be necessary to rest for 5 minutes before a further sprint set was completed. This is because it is necessary for the pulse to return to a resting level between sets to avoid over exertion. It also helps prevent any unnecessary muscle soreness created through overstretching muscles which had become unnecessarily fatigued. Taking an adequate rest and recovery is often underestimated. You should, therefore, ensure that you exercise care when deciding upon your own rest and recovery times.

Over training can be avoided by **adapting** the levels of frequency, intensity and duration within your training. Any of these three factors could result in overtraining. Regularly reviewing and monitoring your performance and completing a training diary, which records your thoughts about the effectiveness of your training, should be helpful in identifying which (if any) of these three factors could best be adapted to reduce the effects of over training.

 Describe for one activity in your Standard Grade course how you could adapt training to ensure that the dangers of over training were avoided.

Setting intensity levels for different exercises

When sprint training to improve anaerobic fitness, you need to train at a high level of intensity for shorter periods. During this anaerobic type of training, you will develop the capacity to cope with the build up of lactic acid, which is produced by the body as a consequence of using anaerobic respiration to provide energy. This level of work can only be sustained for a short period. After a while, oxygen debt will lead to a high level of lactic acid build up with the result that your muscles will tire and begin to work less effectively. For this reason lactate tolerance training programmes are completed by performers in many activities.

 Describe for one activity in your Standard Grade course how you could set intensity levels to ensure that physical fitness training was specific to your needs.

Reversibility

If you stop training then your body will revert to the condition it was in before you began training. The time this takes to occur will be dependent upon how long you trained for. If your training has been short and only over a few weeks then the training benefits will only last for a few weeks before reversibility occurs. For training which takes place over many months the training benefits last for a longer period. This is because fitness adaptation takes a long time to establish. Once it has been established it takes a longer time before regression occurs.

Methods / types of training

For your training to be effective you also need to link the principles of training to appropriate methods of training.

Physical fitness training methods

The most important methods of training for physical fitness are: continuous training, fartlek training, circuit training, weight training and interval fitness training. These methods are described in detail on the following pages.

Continuous training

Includes

- any exercises (e.g. running, swimming and cycling) that ensure that the heart rate is operating in your training zone for approximately 20 to 30 minutes for three to four sessions per week

Venue

- indoor, outdoor or pool-based

Benefits

- develops cardiorespiratory endurance
- develops aerobic capacity
- straightforward to plan
- progressive overload achieved by exercising more often (increasing frequency), by exercising faster (increasing intensity), or by training for longer (increasing duration)

Fartlek training

Includes

- continuous running or swimming with short sprint bursts followed by a slower recovery and then more continuous paced running or swimming

Venue

- indoor, outdoor or pool-based

Benefits

- develops aerobic fitness (e.g. by continuous running) linked to training zone requirements; develops anaerobic fitness (e.g. by short, speed-endurance sprints)
- can be varied to suit your own requirements; can be adapted to terrain (e.g. using short hills for speed endurance sprints during a longer aerobic run)
- progressive overload achieved by exercising more often (frequency), by exercising faster (intensity) or by exercising for longer (duration)

Interval fitness training

Includes

- any form of exercise that allows a work / rest interval to be easily calculated (e.g. swimming, provided that you can swim reasonably well). It is important that the exercises you choose are not ones that you find technically difficult. If they are, your technical limitations will make fitness improvement and measurement difficult.

Venue

- indoor, outdoor or pool-based

Benefits

- enables high intensity work to be undertaken with limited fatigue occurring. For example, a running training programme for the 1500 m could use 4 x 400 m repetitions, completed in 60 seconds with 90 seconds recovery. This causes less fatigue than a single 1500 m run. Running times could be worked out using the same percentage figures used in the weight training example: cardiorespiratory endurance work involving longer distances would be based on 40% to 50% of fastest time.

- develops both aerobic and anaerobic capacity

- progressive overload achieved by carrying out the programme more often (frequency), by working faster or by decreasing rest intervals (intensity) or by exercising for longer (duration)

Interval fitness training

Includes exercises that allow a work / rest interval to be worked out easily. Interval fitness training is useful because it allows you to work hard (at high intensity) followed by periods of rest. This helps you to work for a long time (long duration) without getting too tired.

The type of running shown in the diagram below is a good form of interval training. You jog for 30m then run for 40m at 50% of your fastest speed, then run for 50m at 75% of your fastest speed. After this you go back to jogging. This allows you time to recover. The distance involved as you go 'round the triangle' builds up. So as you keep running, this type of interval training becomes useful for developing cardiorespiratory endurance.

Diagram 2.6

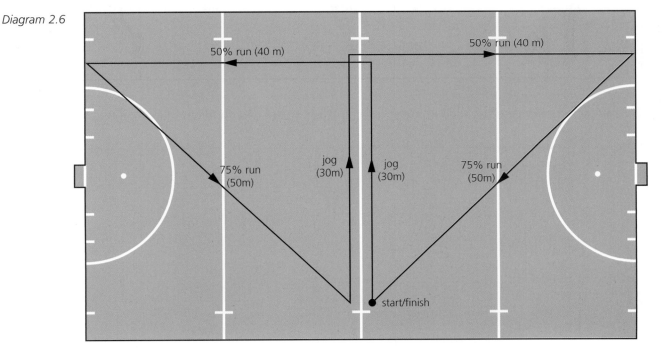

Circuit training

Includes

- fixed circuit of set tasks or individual circuit based on individual's requirements
- multi-station circuit. Stations could include specific or general exercises (e.g. bench jumps, squat thrusts and sit ups)
- general exercises alternating between different major muscle areas
- planned circuit focusing on specific fitness development

Venue

- indoor: general purpose hall with minimum of equipment, mats and benches
- outdoor: open area, possibly with some specific equipment (e.g. rugby balls)

Benefits

- develops both general and specific fitness
- Bench Jumps – Single bench 30 steps x 5 minutes (develops general cardiorespiratory endurance)

  In this example of circuit training to develop the thigh muscles, progressive overload can be achieved by decreasing rest intervals or by increasing repetitions of exercises. Results of times taken or of number of repetitions can be recorded easily.

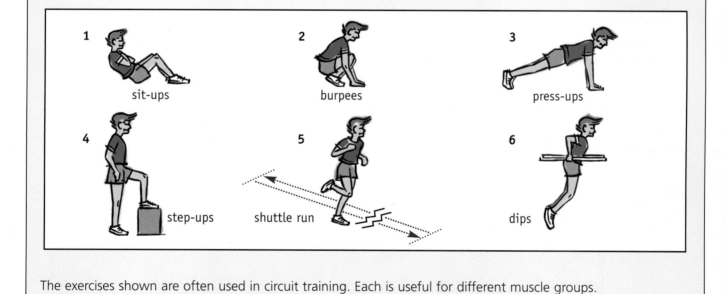

The exercises shown are often used in circuit training. Each is useful for different muscle groups.

Flexibility training

Includes

- forms of flexibility or mobility exercises which allow active or passing stretching or resistance. It is important that the exercises you choose are not ones that you find technically difficult and that you exercise within a range of movement which you can manage. Avoid over stretching.

Venue

- usually indoor or outdoor

Benefits

- enables exercises to be completed which are designed to increase a range of movement around a joint. Practice at moving slowly into exercises and holding the end position for 5 seconds adds to the benefit of each exercise. The practice of stretching and then actively contracting muscles at the end of a mobility exercise enable stretching which is greater and less painful to develop.

- increase a range of movement around a joint

- progressive overload achieved by carrying out the programme more often (frequency), by working at more advanced and demanding stretching exercises (intensity) or by exercising for longer (duration)

Choose two different physical aspects of fitness (cardiorespiratory endurance, local muscular endurance, strength endurance, speed endurance, strength, speed, power, flexibility). Explain which forms of training would be most effective to use for improving the two physical aspects of fitness chosen.

Weight training

Includes

- isotonic exercises in which you move the weight through the range of movement required. In a shoulder press you move from a short bent arm start to a fully straight arm out finish. Useful for developing dynamic strength.

- isometric exercises in which you hold and resist against the weight. Isometric exercises are less common than isotonic. They are useful on occasion for developing static strength. One example is holding a press-up position close to the ground for a number of seconds, and so resisting against your own body weight.

- free-standing weights and weight machines can be used for both isotonic and isometric exercises

Venue

- indoor: weight machines tend to be located in specially designed fitness suites; free-standing weights can often be used in a gymnasium or practice hall

Benefits

- develops both general and specific muscles

- develops muscular endurance as well as strength and power

- straightforward to calculate personal values for exercises (e.g. 40% to 50% of your maximum single lift if based on sets and repetitions for muscular endurance)

    In a general muscular endurance exercise, values for a shoulder press could be 2 sets of 20 repetitions at 25kg. The same exercise could use values of 1 set of 15 repetitions at 45 kg if it was being used as a part of a strength- or power-based circuit. This figure could be calculated on 80% of a maximum single lift.

- progressive overload achieved by increasing weight (intensity) or by increasing repetition (frequency)

Describe for all the different activities in your Standard Grade course, which methods of training would be most effective for your specific physical fitness needs.

Training within activities

To develop **physical fitness** you can either train through a **conditioning** approach (training through activity) or by completing a **fitness training** programme outside the activity (for example by completing a circuit- or weight-training programme). Both types of training are valid provided they follow certain principles. Relevant training methods for physical fitness programmes are explained on pages 68 and 71. By training through the activity you have the chance to improve physical fitness and skills and techniques at the same time.

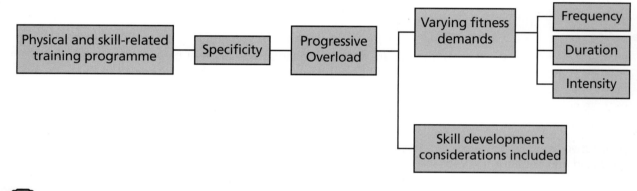

CREDIT GRADE EXTENSION
Training within activities

The diagram below is an example of a conditioning exercise. This could be used by a hockey player in order to develop his or her speed as well as his or her other hockey skills, such as dribbling.

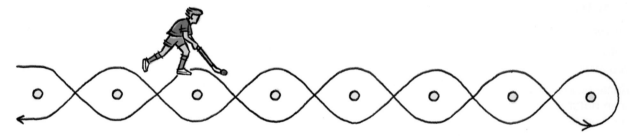

In a conditioning programme for football (see diagram below), you could add progressive overload by increasing the time that you worked on different skill-related practices. An example of this is a goalkeeper completing a 'reaction drill' for longer. This would make it progressively more demanding for the goalkeeper when training.

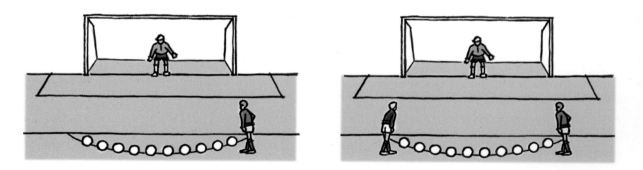

For one activity in your Standard Grade course; describe a conditioning practice which would be useful for improving physical fitness and skills and techniques at the same time.

SECTION 3
SKILLS AND TECHNIQUES

3 SKILLS AND TECHNIQUES

Skills and techniques

A skill describes the purpose of linked sequences of movement. Technique describes the ways of completing a skill.

In volleyball, serving is a skill. Low and high serves are techniques for serving.

(illustration)	Skill: Serving	Technique: Underarm serve
(illustration)	Skill: Serving	Technique: Overhead serve

Skills should be carried out with **maximum efficiency** and performed with the **minimum of effort**. This means skills and techniques can be completed without becoming physically tired. A skilful performer is one who can control physical movement and can **anticipate** what is going to happen next as different skills and techniques are completed.

Study closely the table tennis player.

Observe:

- The balanced standing position, low centre of gravity, wide base of support
- Eyes watching ball closely
- Fine control in completing return shot - a backhand topspin shot is a complex shot

 For different activities in your Standard Grade course, discuss the different major skills and techniques involved.

 Choose **one** skill from **one** activity in your Standard Grade course. Explain the benefits of performing the chosen skill with maximum efficiency and the minimum of effort.

Effects of skills and techniques on performance

Simple (basic) skills are composed of physical actions which are common to many activities such as kicking, jumping, striking, throwing, stretching and rotating. You learn these basic skills (moves) as you grow. This is one reason why taking part in a varied range of physical activities is so useful for your later sporting development.

Your skill level will affect how well you can refine skills through practice, use skills at the correct time, and make decisions about when to use basic and complex (more difficult) skills.

Examples from different activities

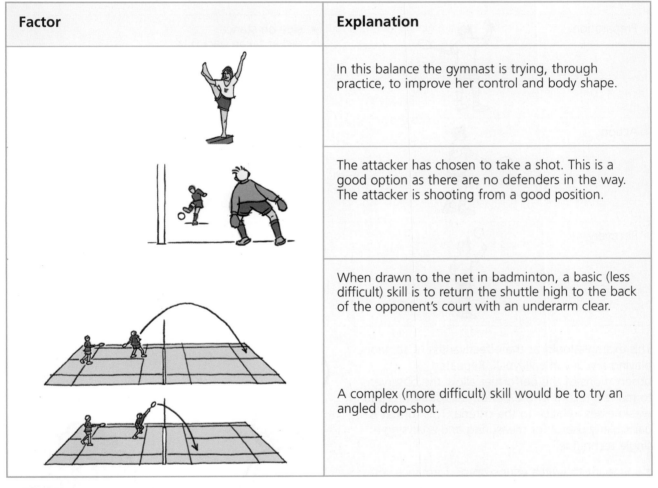

Factor	Explanation
	In this balance the gymnast is trying, through practice, to improve her control and body shape.
	The attacker has chosen to take a shot. This is a good option as there are no defenders in the way. The attacker is shooting from a good position.
	When drawn to the net in badminton, a basic (less difficult) skill is to return the shuttle high to the back of the opponent's court with an underarm clear. A complex (more difficult) skill would be to try an angled drop-shot.

 Study the footballer dribbling using the inside of the right foot and outside of the left foot for control. What effects on performance occur when control of the ball with the outside of the left foot is used?

The added difficulty of dribbling with the outside of the left foot results in the player having to watch the ball more closely. This means it is less likely that the player will be able to watch the movements of other team players and opposing players as closely as necessary.

Choose **one** skill from **one** activity in your Standard Grade course. Explain how you have refined the skill through practice.

3 SKILLS AND TECHNIQUES TECHNIQUES

Preparation / action / recovery

One effective approach for measuring your technique is through analysing your preparation, action and recovery. This means that you analyse the beginning, middle and finish of how well a technique is completed. This format is particularly useful for measuring and analysing a **single technique**.

The first step in using this approach is to **establish the criteria** you wish to use for analysing your technique. Here is an example of criteria for a low serve in badminton.

Factor		Criteria
Preparation		• side-on stance • racket taken back • feet apart
Action		• transfer weight forward • smooth swing gradually getting quicker • drop shuttle, hit below waist
Recovery		• high racket follow-through • ready to react and move to play next shot

This example looks at the effectiveness of someone playing a volley in volleyball. Repeated observations of the performer allow the observer to make a record of the performer's strengths and weaknesses, relative to the criteria. This format is particularly useful for measuring and analysing a single technique.

If you want to watch your own performance you can do this by recording it on video. You can then watch the tape and complete the marking criteria.

Video is useful because it allows you to view a performance many times. It also allows slow motion replay, which is an advantage when the normal speed of a performance makes observation difficult.

STANDARD GRADE & INTERMEDIATE 1 PHYSICAL EDUCATION COURSE NOTES

Study the following table, giving two examples of Preparation, Action and Recovery for each skill / technique shown.

Activity	Gymnastics	Badminton	Basketball
Skill / Technique	Forward Roll	High Serve	Jump Shot
Preparation 1	Feet together	Stand 'side on'	Feet together
Preparation 2	Head tucked in	Take racket back	Look at target
Action 1	Take weight on hands	Transfer w8 forward	Controlled jump
Action 2	Keep legs together	Smooth racket swing	Release at full Height
Recovery 1	Open out carefully	High follow-through	Land in balance
Recovery 2	Finish standing still	Be ready for next shot	React to shot result

Choose three different skills / techniques from three different activities in your Standard Grade course. For each skill or technique give two examples of preparation, action and recovery.

3 SKILLS AND TECHNIQUES
TECHNIQUES

Overcoming problems in skill learning

When you practise skills, you want to improve. It is frustrating if you have difficulty overcoming problems in learning skills and when you appear to be making no apparent progress.

The first step to making skill training effective is to identify your performance strengths and weaknesses. This will help identify any specific improvements in skills / techniques required.

Comparing your ability with a classmate's ability may be useful for establishing your own relative strengths and weaknesses. At other times it may be useful to compare your performance in a particular sport with that of a high level performer, for example, a student competing at a national level in that sport.

Analysing model performers highlights all that a performance includes, for example, the fitness needs of performance, the exact requirements of different skills and the effectiveness of the model performer's decision-making. You can then compare your performance against the model performance.

This is an example from a forehand smash in table tennis:

Description of a forehand smash		Model performance	Your performance
	• Almost side-on start	✓	✓
	• Move bat forwards and upwards	✓	?
	• Hit ball at top of bounce	✓	?
	• Transfer weight forward	✓	✓
	• Square-on finish with upper body facing forward	✓	✓

Comparing performance with the model performance highlights that specific practice to overcome skill weaknesses should focus most on 'moving bat forwards and upwards' and 'hitting ball at top of bounce'.

 Choose one skill from one activity in your Standard Grade course. Explain how you have overcome problems in skill learning through practice.

Skill learning environments

High quality practice for a short time is better than long periods of repeating the same practice. Therefore, to improve your skills and techniques you need to ensure that the 'skill learning environment' is correct for the practices you are completing.

The diagrams below show one example of how you could apply your current level of performance to making effective practices for skill training. The players in light shirts are practising their skills for keeping possession in football. As the players move from practice 1 to practice 2 and then to practice 3, the level of difficulty increases.

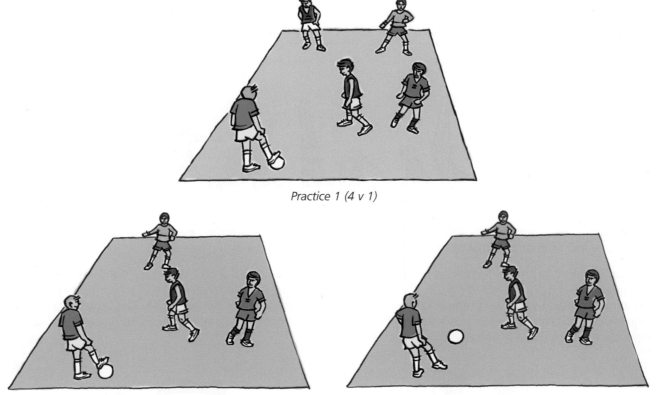

Practice 1 (4 v 1)

Practice 2 (3 v 1)   *Practice 3 (3 v 1, one-touch)*

To ensure the 'skill learning environment' is correct for you would involve joining whichever of the three practices most suited your ability. If you started with the most demanding practice (practice 3) and found it too difficult your passing and control would not improve as much as you would like. It would be better to start with either practice 1 or 2 and progress as your ability improves.

Choose **one** skill practice from **one** activity in your Standard Grade course. Explain how you could simplify the practice to make it less demanding and extend the practice to make it more demanding.

Remember!

- *Skill describes the **purpose** of linked sequences of movements.*

- *Technique is a **way** of executing a skill.*

- *Skills and techniques vary in difficulty according to their requirements, your ability and your previous experience.*

- *'Preparation – Action – Recovery' is an effective way of analysing skills and techniques.*

CREDIT GRADE EXTENSION
Skills and techniques

Skill is **relative** to ability. Your ability to play in defence at hockey determines the type of technique you can use efficiently and the type of options you can use successfully during game play. Your technique and options will probably be less extensive than those of an international hockey player, but more extensive than those of someone just beginning to learn the activity.

> Consider the pictures of the gymnast below who is completing a number of complex techniques in their floor sequence. Identify those techniques which are complex.

The 100 m sprinter requires the ability to repeat straightforward repetitions of sets of movements which require a relatively low level of **co-ordination** and **decision-making**.

The rugby player has more decisions to make as he attempts to protect the ball as well as 'hand-off' the defender who is trying to tackle him. In addition, the attacker has to have **awareness** of where other players are in his team and whether attempting to pass or retain possession is the better option. The attacker also requires co-ordination to retain possession of the ball as well as handing off the tackler. The rugby player has more decisions to make at the one time than the sprinter.

A rugby union player 'handing-off' an opponent

A sprinter in action

Complex skills require more information processing than simple basic skills as they are more intricate. For this reason they require more time to learn and more specific training to develop.

> For the different activities in your Standard Grade course explain the simple and complex skills required for effective performance.

Skill learning

Learning skills involves considering safe practice, methods of practice and how best to practise with a partner and in a group.

Safe practice

When learning skills you need to ensure practice is safe. This will involve you ensuring practice is at the right level for your ability and completing a warm up before practice and a warm down after practice.

It also involves you understanding and abiding by the safety rules which suit the specific activities in which you are participating. In swimming, these include the procedures for stopping swimming and moving to the pool side which have been set out by your teacher. In addition, when swimming in lanes with other class mates you need to follow the agreed rules for when to start swimming, which side of the lane to swim on and when and how overtaking is possible.

A swimmer in lane

You also need to follow more general pool safety issues. These include avoiding running around the pool and following instructions about where diving into the pool is not possible.

A further safe practice issue involves working co-operatively with your partner. In life-saving it is important both for safe and effective practice that you try to work with the rescuer if you are being life saved and vice versa.

A life saver towing a cooperative swimmer in need

 Explain the major safety rules for safe participation in the different activities in your Standard Grade course which take place in gymnasium, games hall and playing fields.

Practice methods

Three main practice methods are: Gradual Build-up, Whole / Part / Whole and Passive / Active practices

Gradual build-up

Gradual build-up is a useful practice method for learning complex (difficult) skills. An example of this is learning a flight dive in swimming:

Stage	Explanation
Stage 1: the sitting dive	• Sit at the edge of the pool. • Bend forward and tuck your head in. • Topple forward and push with your legs. • Reach forward keeping your head down and your backside up.
Stage 2: the kneeling dive	• Start in a slightly higher position than in the sitting dive with one knee on the ground. • Again, topple forward and push with your legs. • You are slightly less rounded than in the sitting dive.
Stage 3: the flight dive	• Bend over in a comfortable flexed position. • Swing your arms forwards as you drive out hard with your legs. • Reach out and dive out as far as you can. • Aim to make as little splash on entry as possible.

By using gradual build-up, you can make the practice more demanding in small steps. This allows you to develop confidence. Practices should be challenging yet **achievable**. They should be geared to your level of performance in order to be valuable and realistic.

You can also add to the demands of gradual build-up practices by changing the level of opposition. For example, in stage 1 overleaf, the defence is weak since there is only one defender to get past. In stage 2, there are three defenders to get past and so the demand (degree of opposition) of this stage is higher. In stage 3, since the defenders can move in all directions, the demand is higher still.

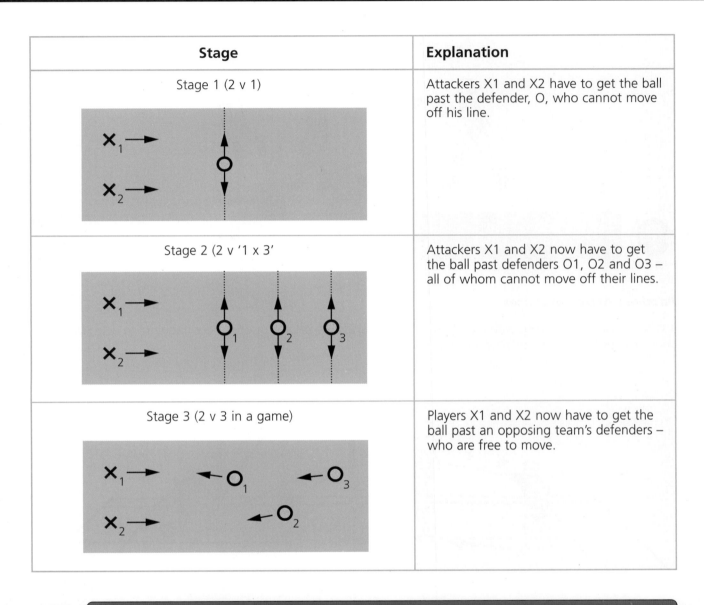

Stage	Explanation
Stage 1 (2 v 1)	Attackers X1 and X2 have to get the ball past the defender, O, who cannot move off his line.
Stage 2 (2 v '1 x 3'	Attackers X1 and X2 now have to get the ball past defenders O1, O2 and O3 – all of whom cannot move off their lines.
Stage 3 (2 v 3 in a game)	Players X1 and X2 now have to get the ball past an opposing team's defenders – who are free to move.

 For the different activities in your Standard Grade course, describe skills and techniques which would benefit from gradual build-up practices.

Whole / Part / Whole

Whole / Part / Whole is often used by performers who already have some experience of the activity. It works best when you can perform the whole skill already.

From your analysis of your performance, you can work out your strengths and weaknesses. Your weaknesses can be improved on in parts on their own. Once performance weaknesses have been improved, the whole skill can then be performed again. Skills which allow parts of the performance to be **separated** easily from the whole performance are the easiest to improve using whole / part / whole methods.

For example, when spiking in volleyball, you may have the weakness that when you jump up high to spike, you travel forward and touch the net. Practising running forward for a few steps and jumping up may be useful before returning to a volleyball game in which the whole spiking action is used.

 For the different activities in your Standard Grade course, describe skills and techniques which would benefit from whole / part / whole practices.

Passive / Active practices

It is often useful to practise with a partner as they can vary the degree of opposition required to help you improve. Consider the badminton practice below.

In this practice the server serves low with the aim of playing an attacking shot from the return to the serve. In the beginning the class mate can return the serve to help the server see how an effective low serve can link to the chance to play a smash shot later. The class mate is providing passive opposition. As the quality of service improves the class mate can play more demanding service returns. The class mate is now providing more active opposition.

 For the different activities in your Standard Grade course, describe skills and techniques which would benefit from passive / active practices.

CREDIT GRADE EXTENSION
Skill learning

Stages of learning

There are **three important stages** in learning and developing skills: these are often referred to as the Planning Stage, the Practice Stage and the Automatic Stage. For your credit grade Standard Grade studies, you require to understand in detail the automatic stage of skill learning. Information on the Planning and Practice stages is provided as background information to help you to see how progression to the automatic stage of skill learning occurs.

The Planning Stage

During the planning stage, you find out what the skill involves. You establish what the parts of the skill are and make your first attempts at learning each part. Errors are likely to be common at this stage in learning, so you will need advice, encouragement, and support to make progress.

Planning Stage – Basketball Example
<ul><li>you make a slow approach</li><li>you get used to moving towards the basket (through jogging)</li><li>you jump up and try to place the ball on the back-board</li><li>you make quite a lot of errors – when the ball misses the back-board or when you lose control of the ball when jumping up</li><li>you take advice from teachers / friends</li></ul>

The Practice Stage

During the practice stage you **link together** all the required parts of the skill. Simple skills will require less practice than complex skills. Quality practice will reduce the number of mistakes made during performance.

Practice Stage – Basketball Example
<ul><li>your jump is balanced</li><li>you place the ball accurately on the back-board</li><li>you make fewer errors, although some refinement is still needed</li></ul>

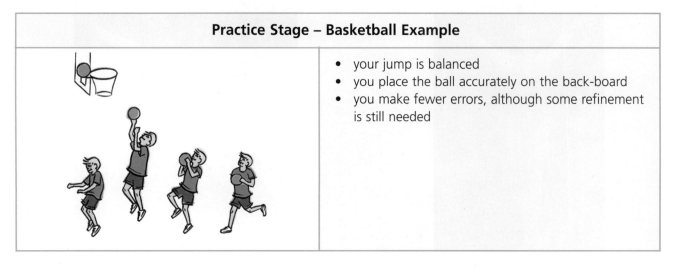

3 SKILLS AND TECHNIQUES
WAYS OF DEVELOPING SKILL

The Automatic Stage

At this stage, errors are less likely and most key parts of a skill have become automatic. As a result, little attention is paid to them. For example, at the automatic stage in volleyball during a dig you can move to the ball in balance, link your arms correctly and lower your centre of gravity automatically. Due to your higher skill level you can give closer attention to more detailed aspects of your performance. For example, in your volleyball dig you are now able to concentrate on the speed of the dig to your setter as well as on the direction and flight path of the shot.

Automatic Stage – Basketball Example	
	• you make a medium-fast approach • you jump up high with the ball securely held • you angle the ball accurately onto the back-board to score • you make very few errors • most of your lay-up shots result in a basket scored

> Choose one skill from an activity in your Standard Grade course. Explain, in detail, the characteristics of performance at each stage of skill learning.

Principles of effective practice and refinement

For your practice to be effective you should set clear **objectives**. This will enable you to refine performance. You must consider your existing level of ability and current strengths and weaknesses at the beginning, when setting targets for performance improvement practice.

Compare the two gymnasts on the beam. They are both practising techniques which suit their ability.

A gymnast completing a basic balance on the beam

A gymnast completing a complex demanding jump on the beam

You should practise a difficult technique (such as completing a jump on the beam) when you are ready. Practice before you are ready will often result in limited or no improvements.

It might also affect your level of motivation in unhelpful ways. It is important that your objectives are achievable. This helps keep your motivation levels high.

Choose one technique from an activity in your Standard Grade course. Explain your objectives for improving this technique and your performance targets.

Another principle of effective practice is that you train for a suitable **training time**. Too short and improvements will be limited. Too long and you may become fatigued and prone to picking up an injury. Training for too long a time can also lead to boredom and a gradual reduction in the amount of progress you make. Having **varied practices** is one effective way of **reducing boredom**. In swimming, for example, varying the strokes you are swimming can make practice more enjoyable and motivate you to keep practising.

Choose one technique from an activity in your Standard Grade course. Explain how you could vary practices to reduce the possibility of boredom occurring.

The correct training time will depend upon the demands of the activity. For some activities such as swimming and for longer distance running events in athletics training times are usually long. For other activities, such as throwing and sprinting events in athletics, training times tend to be shorter.

Longer training times

Shorter training times

Training time will also depend on your **level of ability**. When you are a beginner you tend to practise for less time than if you are a more able performer. If you are practising long distance running events your training time will increase as your ability increases.

3 SKILLS AND TECHNIQUES
WAYS OF DEVELOPING SKILL

Work-to-rest ratio

When training you need to calculate the ratio of work relative to rest. Working out this ratio is one of the key issues in making skill training specific to your needs. The work-to-rest ratio takes into account:

▸ your previous experience in the activity

▸ your level of practical ability

▸ the difficulty of the skill involved

▸ the physical demands involved in the practice

 Choose one technique from an activity in your Standard Grade course. Explain how you set the work-to-rest ratio to ensure practice was effective.

 ## CREDIT GRADE EXTENSION
Principles of effective practice and refinement

Practising under pressure

With skills and techniques that you can complete with a high degree of control and fluency it is important to complete practice under pressure. This will make practice relate to performing in competition. In team activities this could involve increasing the demands of opponents.

Practising under pressure can also involve individual indirectly competitive and non-competitive activities such as swimming and gymnastics. In indirectly competitive activities, such as a 100 m front crawl race in swimming, you can often practise with another swimmer beside you. This adds to the pressure of performing. In indirectly non-competitive activities such as gymnastics, practising a floor sequence in front of an audience can add to the pressure, but also make practice realistic for the performance goals you have set.

 Choose one skill from an activity in your Standard Grade course. Explain, in detail, the principles of effective practice you have considered in setting clear objectives for skill training. Your answer should make clear references to training times, variation in practices, work-to-rest training intervals and any pressure practices you used.

Feedback

Feedback is information you collect about your performance. For example, in golf you need to take in feedback about important factors that can affect how well you play the hole. For the hole shown below, these factors include the strength of the wind, the bunkers, the river across the fairway and the trees beside the green.

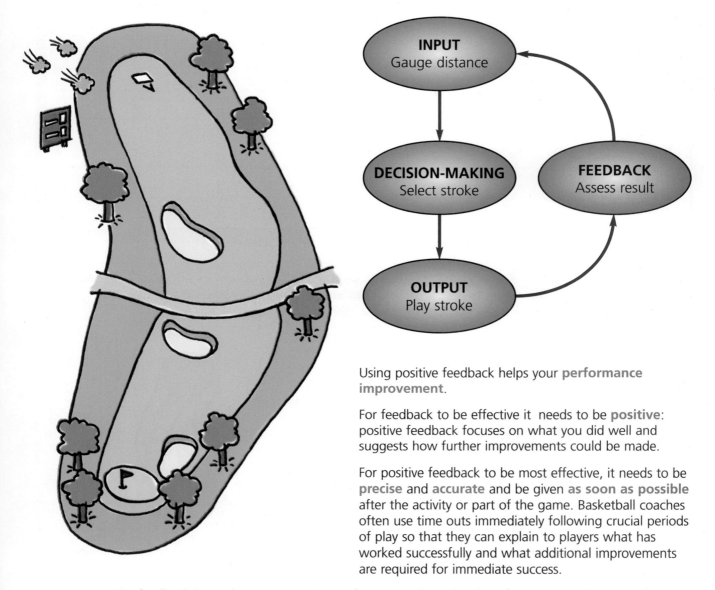

Using positive feedback helps your **performance improvement**.

For feedback to be effective it needs to be **positive**: positive feedback focuses on what you did well and suggests how further improvements could be made.

For positive feedback to be most effective, it needs to be **precise** and **accurate** and be given **as soon as possible** after the activity or part of the game. Basketball coaches often use time outs immediately following crucial periods of play so that they can explain to players what has worked successfully and what additional improvements are required for immediate success.

You can receive feedback by evaluating your own performance, through advice from your teacher and also by receiving advice from a class mate. You will often work with a class mate or partner on your Standard Grade course.

When offering feedback, try to focus on the most important points necessary for improvement and identify specific strengths and weaknesses. Comparing observed performance against criteria on checklists is one popular method for providing feedback.

When working with a partner feedback can be provided in various ways. You can talk with your class mate (verbal), note down the key points needing improvements (written) and inform them of the results of their performance (knowledge of results). The example overleaf shows the results of a small-sided hockey game lasting 30 minutes each half where results of about dribbling, tackling and shooting has been collected.

3 SKILLS AND TECHNIQUES
WAYS OF DEVELOPING SKILL

Game Analysis Sheet

Team: Scotstown Academy
Opposition: Central High School

Role: Attacker
Date: 25/11/05

✓ = effective   ✗ = ineffective

Time (minutes)	Dribbling	Tackling	Shooting
1st half 0–10	✓	✓	
11–19	✗	✓✗	✓
21–30	✓✗	✓	✗
2nd half 0–10		✓	✓
11–19			✗
21–30	✗		

From the results in the diagram what feedback would you offer the performer? Specifically, what skill do they appear most effective at? What skill are they least effective at? Are they most involved in the game during the first or second half?

As well as being provided with feedback about your performance you can evaluate your performance through the **internal** feedback you receive. This is easier to do as your performance level improves. Internal feedback is often referred to as 'kinaesthetic awareness' and refers to the 'feel' of different sporting actions. For example, in basketball as your ability improves the more able you are likely to be at 'feeling' whether the shot is on target or off.

A basketball player completing a jump shot

For the different activities in your Standard Grade course, describe one skill or technique where **verbal** feedback would be useful.

For the different activities in your Standard Grade course, describe one skill or technique where **written** feedback would be useful.

For the different activities in your Standard Grade course, describe one skill or technique where **knowledge of results** feedback would be useful.

Co-operation

In the different activities in your Standard Grade course it is important that you can effectively co-operate with class mates. This involves **co-operating when performing**. The setter in volleyball has to co-operate with the player spiking the ball. This involves practising together and talking about how best the set and spike can be completed.

Co-operation also involves observing a partner and **recording information**. This involves being a critical friend to your partner and team mates. You watch and note down information carefully and offer feedback on specific skills and general encouragement. You develop trust with your partner.

When participating as part of a team working co-operatively involves **accepting responsibility** and recognising your role within a team. In basketball, in a zone defence it is important that you co-operate with others to keep the correct shape for your team as a unit.

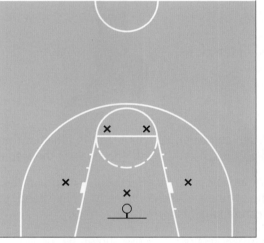

For the different activities in your Standard Grade course, describe one practice where you have co-operated effectively with a partner when performing.

For the different activities in your Standard Grade course, describe one practice where you have co-operated effectively with a partner when recording information about performance.

For the different activities in your Standard Grade course, describe one practice when accepting responsibility within a team has been important for effective performance.

Balance

Balance is the ability to retain the centre of gravity over your base of support. Balancing requires the control of different groups of muscles. The exact muscle requirements depend upon the nature of the task. Static balances such as a headstand in gymnastics require you to hold a balance, while dynamic balances require you to maintain balance under constantly changing conditions. When skiing you constantly adjust your dynamic balance as you travel over changing terrain in order to remain in balance.

When completing a sprint start in athletics the centre of gravity is over the base of support. Most of the weight is on the athletes' arms. This enables them to drive off their leading (front) foot when hearing the start signal.

For technique to be effective it is helpful if the major muscles involved in balances have good body tension. For the gymnast above completing a headstand, tense stomach and leg muscles help maintain the balance. Their posture benefits from body tension.

Effective technique is also shown by the gymnast's large base of support when completing the headstand. The triangle shape created by the placement of forehead and hands helps improve performance.

 A headstand is a less difficult technique than a handstand. Can you suggest two reasons why this is the case?

A handstand: A demanding technique

In the handstand the centre of gravity is higher and the base of support is smaller.

In the headstand the centre of gravity is lower and the base of support is larger.

The greater **stability** provided by the lower centre of gravity and larger base of support in the headstand makes it easier to control the movements into and out of the balance. For this reason when learning the headstand you can move to a tucked headstand position first. When you are in control of your movements to this point you can slowly use the benefits of your stable base of support and low centre of gravity to extend and straighten your legs. Good body tension should help ensure your stay in balance

Which of these three balances is most stable?

The gymnast completing the side splits in a sitting position is most stable. Her low centre of gravity and the large base of support in contact with the ground ensure that remaining in balance is relatively straightforward.

The gymnast completing the balance where their full weight is taken on both hands is a complex challenging balance. The base of support is quite small and her centre of gravity is difficult to maintain over the base of support.

The two gymnasts completing a pairs balance is the most difficult. This is due to small base of support for both gymnasts and through the lack of stability in the base of support.

 For the different activities in your Standard Grade course, describe one technique which requires effective static balance. Explain how you moved into and out of the balance safely.

For the different activities in your Standard Grade course, describe one technique which requires effective dynamic balance. Explain how you controlled your movements to remain in balance.

Transfer of weight

For a whole variety of different skills and techniques you need to transfer your weight for effective performance. At times, this can be in single actions such as throwing the javelin. At other times, for example when running, simple actions are repeated.

How well you transfer your weight involves considering how well balanced you are when performing. Consider the swimmer completing a dive entry to the pool. As their centre of gravity moves outside their base of support and they begin to lose balance they drive and extend the legs and reach forward for a streamline entry to the dive.

The hockey player in this corner practice requires to transfer their weight from the back to front foot and they push the pass quickly to their team mates.

A hockey player about to take a short corner

For the different activities in your Standard Grade course, describe one technique which requires a single transference of weight.

For the different activities in your Standard Grade course, describe one technique which requires a repeated transference of weight.

Application of force

When performing different skills and techniques different forces are applied and resisted.

For every action there is an equal and opposite reaction (Newton's Third Law). For the shot putter in athletics there will be an equal reaction on the throwing hand. For the footballer who is shooting there will be an equal reaction on the foot.

A footballer kicking the ball

A shot putter 'putting' the shot

In both of these examples, speed and power are important in applying force. The direction of the force is also important. In the football example the footballer is trying to keep the shot low and close to the ground. For the shot putter there is an optimum angle at which to putt the shot. If the shot putt is released and putted too high or too low the distance thrown will be less. For releasing the shot, an angle between 30 and 45 degrees is likely to be best.

To help performers resist the forces involved in completing different actions various types of equipment are used. Sprinters use starting blocks, outdoor games players use studded boots to provide grip and **resistance**. By contrast, shot putters use chalk dust to **reduce friction** between the throwing hand and the shot so that the throw can be more easily completed.

 For the different activities in your Standard Grade course, describe one technique where there is an equal and opposite reaction to the force applied.

 ## CREDIT GRADE EXTENSION
Application of force

If speed is required then the greater the force applied the better. Differences in the mass of the body will affect performance. If the force applied to the sprinting block is the same the athlete with the smaller mass will accelerate at a quicker rate.

A 100 m sprint race in action

Rotation

In different activities you rotate (turn) in order to carry out effective skills and techniques. When throwing the discus in athletics you turn around in a spinning back-to-front movement to generate power. This is a complex technique. You build up speed before throwing, by quickly turning your feet around. After the throw you follow through and keep turning until you have regained your balance.

As well as rotating around you also can rotate by turning head over heels. This is part of completing a front or back somersault. Another form of rotation is when you turn sideways. A cartwheel, where you turn over from feet to hand balancing on ground before returning to feet on the ground, is an example of this type of rotation.

 For the different activities in your Standard Grade course, describe one technique where rotation is used to enhance performance.

Resistance

When you apply force there will be resistance. This resistance can either be an advantage or a disadvantage. When sprinting in athletics the starting blocks are an advantage. They provide a resistance. The track creates a helpful resistance as you continue running. If you are running into a headwind this would be unhelpful.

Force overcoming resistance is important in swimming. Consider the diagram below.

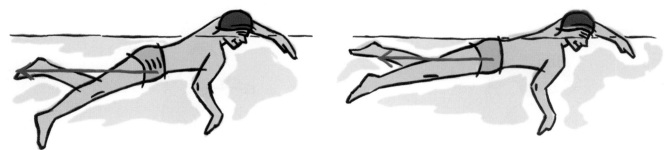

First swimmer   *Second swimmer*

In this example, the first swimmer is having difficulty in swimming effectively due to the resistance created by poor streamlining. This is evident through the swimmer's lower centre of gravity. With the second swimmer the leg action is more effective, less water is displaced, the swimmer's centre of gravity is higher. Overall, the forces applied are overcoming the resistance created by the water in a more effective way.

 In recent years equipment changes have tried to minimise the effects of resistance. Study the picture of the cyclist below. Identify how equipment has been designed to create effective streamlining.

A cyclist competing in a road race

 For the different activities in your Standard Grade course, describe one technique where resistance has helped your performance.

For the different activities in your Standard Grade course, describe one technique where resistance has made your performance more difficult.

For the different activities in your Standard Grade course, describe one technique where improved streamlining has limited the effects of resistance.

Follow through

When completing different skills and techniques it is important that kicking, striking and throwing actions have a good follow through. A good follow through is part of effective performance and follows on from the preparation and action phases in different skills and techniques.

In this football example the follow through is in the direction of the shot. This is similar in the throwing example where the arm follows the intended direction of the throw.

A footballer kicking the ball

A baseball player throwing the ball

In other actions the follow through involves body rotation. The ball and socket joints in the hips and shoulder help rotation in the two different striking actions in tennis and golf shown below.

A tennis player during the action part of the shot (1)

A golfer completing their follow through

A tennis player at the beginning of their recovery (2)

 For the different activities in your Standard Grade course, describe one technique where follow through is important in a **kicking** action.

 For the different activities in your Standard Grade course, describe one technique where follow through is important in a **striking** action.

 For the different activities in your Standard Grade course, describe one technique where follow through is important in a **throwing** action.

SECTION 4
EVALUATING

Evaluating

When evaluating you need to complete two types of task. First, you need to observe and describe accurately what you see. Secondly, you need to suggest improvements to performance.

To observe accurately be clear about what you are expected to watch. For examination answers read questions carefully and ensure your answer is specific to the question. Try to be **objective**. This means answering on exactly what you have observed. When suggesting improvements to performance ensure your answers are **positive**. Describing what someone is doing wrong is not nearly as helpful as suggesting what they require to do to improve.

For both describing actions and suggesting improvements the key to gaining the most possible marks available is to provide **clear**, **detailed** and **accurate** answers. You can make your answer more detailed by identifying the skill such as passing, throwing, rolling, striking, catching and then adding further details about direction, speed and the like.

A good description of this handspring would make reference to the gymnast reaching out with extended arms, the legs staying **extended** as they overtake the arms, both hands striking the mat together, legs landing together. Further description could highlight the extended position in the run up approach, how the arms stay together and extended, and that the run up accelerates to a fast speed with a strong leg swing to generate **rotation**.

A good description of a left handed lay up shot in basketball would make reference to the player moving in towards the basket at a controlled speed which is as fast as possible, taking off on the right foot, jumping as high as possible, laying ball onto backboard and landing on both feet.

Evaluating examination

You will want to ensure that your course revision is rewarded by completing the video examination successfully. The following advice should help you to achieve your goal.

Watch the video closely. The commentary will indicate how many times you will see the action. **Listen carefully** to the commentary. Make sure you watch **each viewing** closely. Ensure that you view when you should. Avoid writing when you should be watching. Sufficient time is available for completing your written answer after you have viewed the different actions.

Parts (a) and (b) of every question ask you to **observe and describe** what different performers are doing and to **suggest improvements**. You need to be careful to avoid answering about what performers are not doing. Negative answers about what performers are doing wrong are not acceptable. Describe accurately what performers are doing and, if required, suggest improvements they could make to their action.

Answer in as much detail as you can. Some answers may be for 3 marks. For these questions, you will need to provide some detailed observations and judgements in your answer. Make it clear what it is you are writing about. For example, if you are suggesting improvements to a Gymnastics sequence which involves different balances, ensure that your answer correctly mentions Balance 1, Balance 2 or Balance 3 as requiring improvement. In this way, your answer contains more specific detail. An answer such as 'keep legs straight' is more likely to gain marks if you can complete it with 'keep legs straight in the second balance'.

Try to avoid being upset by the 'activity focus'. Many different activities are taught in Standard Grade courses – you will probably see questions which use activities which are not part of your course. However, the questions are all general in nature rather than activity-specific.

For example, a question may use Rugby as the activity focus. You may be asked about how well the defenders control the attackers' space. This is the type of detail you will have covered in your course, perhaps not in Rugby but in another activity, for example Basketball. Therefore, try to relate your knowledge and understanding from your experience in one activity to another.

Question – How could the defender try to gain possession of the ball?

Answer – Move towards attacker with ball

How to analyse effectively in Intermediate 1 Level Physical Education

The Cycle of Analysis

The Cycle of Analysis is one popular approach that is useful for analysing and developing your performance as part of your performance improvement programme. Using the Cycle of Analysis, you collect information about your performance in an organised way. In this way you identify and assess specific aspects of your performance.

Study the four stages of the Cycle of Analysis in diagram 5.1.

Diagram 5.1

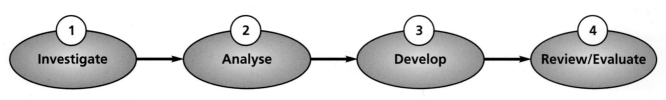

These four stages can be applied effectively to your own activities. Diagram 5.2 below shows the complete cycle of analysis.

Diagram 5.2

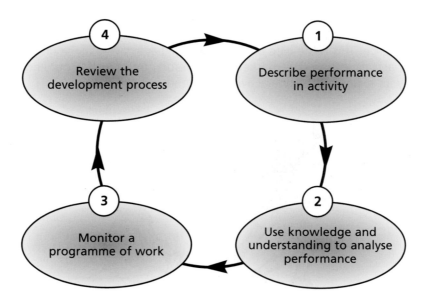

Links between Standard Grade *Course Notes* and Intermediate 1 Physical Education

Performance Appreciation (Area 1)

is a **general** broad view of performance which relates to the three other specific areas of analysis of performance areas. The Key Concepts in this area are:

• Overall nature and demands of quality performance	28-31
• Technical, physical, personal and special qualities of performance	36
• Mental factors influencing performance	63
• Use of appropriate models of performance	76
• Planning and managing personal performance improvement	86-88

Preparation of the Body (Area 2)

is a **specific** analysis of the fitness and training requirements necessary for your performance. The Key Concepts in this area are:

• Fitness assessment in relation to personal performance and the demands of activities	43-63
• Application of different types of fitness in the development of activity specific performance	72
• Physical, skill-related and mental types of fitness	43-63
• Principles and methods of training	65-71
• Planning, implementing and monitoring training	72

Skills and Techniques (Area 3)

is a **specific** analysis of your skills and techniques needs in performance. The Key Concepts in this area are:

• The concept of skill and skilled performance.	74-81
• Skill / technique improvement through mechanical analysis or movement analysis or consideration of quality.	92-98
• The development of skill and the refinement of technique.	82-91

Structures, Strategies and Composition (Area 4)

is a **specific** analysis of the influence of shape, form and design on your performance. The Key Concepts in this area are:

• The structures, strategies and / or compositional elements that are fundamental to activities.	18-27
• Identification of strengths and weaknesses in performance in terms of:	
– roles and relationships, formations, tactical or design elements, choreography and composition	34-35
• Information processing, problem-solving and decision-making when working to develop and improve performance.	32-33

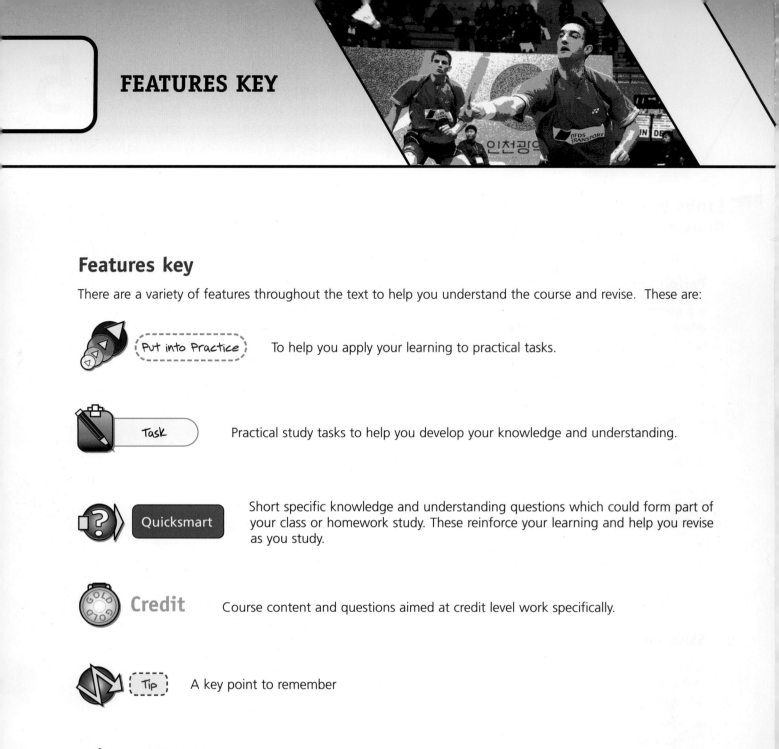

Features key

There are a variety of features throughout the text to help you understand the course and revise. These are:

Put into Practice — To help you apply your learning to practical tasks.

Task — Practical study tasks to help you develop your knowledge and understanding.

Quicksmart — Short specific knowledge and understanding questions which could form part of your class or homework study. These reinforce your learning and help you revise as you study.

Credit — Course content and questions aimed at credit level work specifically.

Tip — A key point to remember

Bigger Picture — A wider ranging question which links across your Course and could form part of your class or homework study.